ELEVATE YOUR LIFE

Exercise Authority Over
The Twelve Spiritual Dimensions

Dr. R. Heard

WESTBOW*
PRESS
A DIVISION OF THOMAS NELSON
& ZONDERVAN

WestBow Press books may be ordered through booksellers or by contacting:

WestBow Press
A Division of Thomas Nelson & Zondervan
1663 Liberty Drive
Bloomington, IN 47403
www.westbowpress.com
1 (866) 928-1240

Because of the dynamic nature of the Internet, any web addresses or links contained in this book may have changed since publication and may no longer be valid. The views expressed in this work are solely those of the author and do not necessarily reflect the views of the publisher, and the publisher hereby disclaims any responsibility for them.

Any people depicted in stock imagery provided by Thinkstock are models, and such images are being used for illustrative purposes only.
Certain stock imagery © Thinkstock.

Manuscript Development – Sally Fuller
Editor – Marcella Willhoite

ISBN: 978-1-4908-5242-3 (sc)
ISBN: 978-1-4908-5241-6 (hc)
ISBN: 978-1-4908-5243-0 (e)

Library of Congress Control Number: 2014916753

Printed in the United States of America.

WestBow Press rev. date: 10/23/2014

ACKNOWLEDGEMENTS

Where do I begin to thank the wonderful people who have helped me with the publication of this book?

First and foremost would be Geri, my wife, who in all our years of ministry has never complained about the time required for me to be both pastor and father to so many others in ministry.

Then there is the church family who has so willingly followed the pursuit of our dream of building an Apostolic House.

I certainly must mention Marcella Willhoite, who faithfully edits my work and makes sure each of my books comes to completion. We also thank her assistant, Sherena Ward, for her many contributions.

Finally, I would be remiss if I failed to give special thanks to the many wonderful people of God, beginning with my grandmother, or "Nanny" as we fondly called her, who taught me so much of what I know about the ways of God.

FOREWORD

The Christian life is full of adventure. The greatest adventure upon which you will ever embark is when you abandon self and pursue the higher passion of following where the God of the universe leads. Sometimes the road is rough with hairpin turns, but it always leads to an elevated commitment, a more complete surrender, and a joy beyond description.

God wants to elevate your life. As the basis for this teaching, I have chosen the following verse, although many others throughout Scripture will confirm this theory:

> *"But because of His great love for us, God, who is rich in mercy, made us alive with Christ even when we were dead in transgressions— it is by grace you have been saved. And God RAISED US UP with Christ and seated us with Him in the HEAVENLY realms in Christ Jesus, in order that in the coming ages He might show the incomparable riches of His grace, expressed in His kindness to us in Christ Jesus,"* (Ephesians 2:4-7 NIV).

Elevation is the natural progression of life when we connect with God. I have never known a person who has connected with Him to complain later that life had become worse than it was before. It just doesn't work that way.

Depending upon your background, elevating your life may require some tweaking of traditions and beliefs. Sections of this book will challenge what you learned in church. I ask that you prayerfully consider what I have to say and not disregard any of it.

Regardless of your background, elevating your life requires action. Elevation only occurs as you break through to successive spiritual dimensions. Two-thirds of this book will involve learning how to exert power and authority in spiritual dimensions.

> *"When Jesus had called the Twelve together, he gave them power and authority to drive out all demons and to cure diseases, and he sent them out to proclaim the kingdom of God and to heal the sick"* (Luke 9:1-2 NIV).

Jesus *"gave them power and authority"* over spiritual dimensions. Each word of that phrase is critical:

- gave: it can't be earned.

- them: that includes you and me!

- power and authority: both are needed to achieve the elevated life God has planned for you.

This book has two sections: an 'instruction manual' for your journey to new heights and an in-depth study of the twelve spiritual dimensions that must be conquered to experience continual elevation. While not an exhaustive list, these dimensions are the twelve God revealed as I prepared for this teaching.

A final word before we begin: our enemy will relentlessly oppose God's plan of elevation. Expect to encounter resistance as you begin breaking through each dimension. Remember, the devil is a defeated enemy whose primary weapon is deception. Truth sends him running. God's Word is your arsenal. When the enemy throws up a roadblock, choose a weapon from your arsenal and blast him with a barrage of scriptural truth. It works every time!

See you at the top!

CONTENTS

INTRODUCTION

Wave Good-Bye to Base Camp!

O n May 18, 1923, the *New York Times* published a story with a phrase, when taken out of context, has become the famous rebuttal to the age-old question: "Why do you climb a mountain?" The seemingly flippant response, "because it's there," was given by British mountain climber George Leigh Mallory to reporters while raising money for his third attempt to reach the summit of Mount Everest, our planet's highest peak. At the time of his remark, no one had ever achieved this seemingly impossible goal.

Mallory's full response to the question was, "Because it's there.....Its existence is a challenge. The answer is instinctive in part, I suppose, of man's desire to conquer the universe."

In context, the serious answer holds much more truth than the trite three-word phrase that has become the pat answer for such questions. Man *does* have an inherent need to overcome challenges, to move forward and upward in his world, and to aspire to new elevations, whether physical, mental, or spiritual.

According to *Mountaineering: The Freedom of the Hills*,[1] which is regarded by many as the "textbook for mountaineering" in North America,[2] the actual sport of mountain climbing requires three things: experience, athletic ability, and technical knowledge to maintain safety. I would add to that list *courage*. Every mountain climber will tell you, it takes more than a little guts to leave the safety of base camp at the foot of a mountain and head into unknown territory.

The many perils of mountain climbing include the obvious:

- falling – either down the mountain or into treacherous crevices

- dehydration

- exhaustion

- altitude sickness (a condition that mimics the flu, produced by lack of oxygen at high altitudes)

- avalanches

- hypothermia….to name a few.

---

[1] Ronald C. Eng (ed) *Mountaineering: The Freedom of the Hills. 8th Ed.* (Mountaineers Books 09/8/2010) ISBN 978-1-59485-137-7.

[2] http://en.wikipedia.org/wiki/Mountaineering: The Freedom of the Hills

Temperatures at Everest's pinnacle average -15 degrees below zero and can plunge to an almost instantly lethal -100 below. During some seasons, the summit of this king of all mountains, stretching 29,029 feet into the air, is continually battered with hurricane force winds.

The fact that men know of these perils, yet are resolutely determined to overcome this and other mountains, is proof that Mallory's assessment may have been correct. Yet, historically, there have been four reasons for climbing mountains:

- Hunt for food. To feed his family, a man would track a deer, bear, or other animal into higher than humanly comfortable elevations, hoping to find enough meat to feed his wife and children through the harsh winter months.

- Spiritual pilgrimages. Buddhist pilgrims have climbed to dangerous heights in the Himalayan Mountains hoping to hear some word of knowledge or wisdom from "holy hermit" monks sitting in temples that would inspire or change their lives—or at least help them descend the mountain safely.

- For sport. In the 19th century, European mountaineers coined the term "Alpinism" to define climbing to difficult heights purely for the fun of it. The accomplishment of reaching new heights and relishing unknown vistas brings the Alpinist great personal satisfaction.

- The mountain stood between them and the place they wanted to be.

Spiritually speaking, Christians pursue higher elevations for the same reasons. A spiritual hunger drives you to push higher in the search for more satisfying spiritual food. The quest for spiritual revelation can motivate a constant strengthening of your relationship with the Father. In each level of relationship, we long for the sheer joy of resting just a moment to take in the view! But, as Mallory pointed out, man has an inherent desire to reach new heights in *all* realms.

The good news is that God wants to take you on a journey to the top! Not just an increased spiritual altitude, but your *entire* life. If He is interested in every part of your life, you can bet He wants to elevate it. In fact, He has already set the plan in motion:

> *"But because of His great love for us, God, who is rich in mercy, made us alive with Christ even when we were dead in transgressions — it is by grace you have been saved. And God RAISED US UP with Christ and seated us with Him in the HEAVENLY realms in Christ Jesus, in order that in the coming ages He might show the incomparable riches of His grace, expressed in His kindness to us in Christ Jesus,"*
> (Ephesians 2:4-7 NIV).

No matter where on the globe you live, 'up' is still up and 'the heavenly realms' is an elevated position. If *God* has raised you, *He* has elevated you. We cannot elevate ourselves; if you are God's child, He has elevated you. The reason for the elevation is to establish us in Christ so that our elevated state will bring Him glory (Ephesians 2:7).

Living perpetually at 'base camp' will never draw the lost to the love of God. The best advertisement for attracting the unsaved into God's Kingdom is happy, blessed people who are already part of His Kingdom. God wants you to be elevated so that people will look at you and say, "Wow! Whatever is going on in your life, I want it in mine!"

Obviously, I have never climbed Mount Everest, although I have seen it when traveling to India or Nepal. Its enormity is almost impossible to describe. By comparison, the Colorado Rocky Mountains would appear as little foothills. You can be sure that those who have managed to reach its zenith will tell you that nothing on earth can compare to that view. It must be absolutely beyond the imagination of those of us who have never been there.

That, my friends, is the view God wants for you! It is far beyond the imagination! Not the view from the summit of Everest—although, who knows, He may have that in store for some of you—but the view from your next . . . and your next . . . and your next level of authority, accomplishment, and accolade. It's time to look over your shoulder and wave good-bye to base camp. God is about to elevate your life!

Chapter 1

GRAB YOUR GEAR!

J ourneys to places like the summit of Mount Everest require months of painstaking conditioning, meticulous timing, and strategic planning. Your journey to new heights in Christ is very similar, so before you begin searching for a mountain to conquer, let's lay some groundwork.

The trip from Everest Base Camp (EBC) to its peak takes between seven and nine weeks, with stops at numerous camps. After that lengthy hike, mountaineers can remain at the peak only for a few wonderful minutes before heading back. Their bodies cannot tolerate such extreme elevation without specialized breathing equipment; but even then, prolonged exposure to extreme elevations is physically harmful.

THE SAME, ONLY DIFFERENT

T wo glaring differences between new God-glorifying heights and the conquest of Mount Everest are the length of the trip and duration of your stay.

Elevation is a lifelong process. As long as you occupy space on planet earth, you will always aspire to new levels of Kingdom elevation. Your upward mobility is determined by your ability to exercise authority in twelve sequential, spiritual dimensions that we'll examine in-depth.

Second, as you reach a new level of elevation, God intends for you to take up residence. Unlike the Everest mountaineers, you won't hang out for a few spectacular moments, slap your companions on the back, snap a few photos, and then head back down. Once you ascend to a new altitude, God wants you to look around, enjoy the view, and then take possession of the new level. You know you're staying because He says so:

> *"And God raised us up with Christ and* **seated** *us with Him in the heavenly realms in Christ Jesus, in order that in the coming ages He might show the incomparable riches of His grace, expressed in His kindness to us in Christ Jesus"* (Ephesians 2:6-7 NIV).

The word *'seated'* indicates you won't soon be running down the slopes. As my grandmother would have said to a welcome guest, "Why don't you sit a spell?" You don't sit unless you have plans to stay a while.

START PACKING

Mountaineers heading out from EBC take basics in their backpacks, such as: sleeping bags, a variety of footwear, lightweight warm clothing, water bottles, and sunglasses or goggles. More specialized climbing equipment would include: karabiners (locking metal hooks); crampons (a piece of metal with sharp points on the bottom of boots to simplify walking on ice and snow); perlon cord; ice axes; a harness; and rappelling devices, to name a few.

Because God intends your promotion to be permanent, it is imperative not only to make the trip, but once there, to possess the land. Just as the Everest climbers have specific equipment, you will need a 'gray matter backpack' of special knowledge and truth to make the climb and take up residence.

The very first thing to load into your backpack is a firm belief that God's plans for your life include elevation. It is essential to the success of your journey. His plans are not merely for your good, they are strategic in nature for the growth of the Kingdom.

> *"'I know the plans I have for you,' declares the Lord. 'Plans to prosper you and not to harm you, plans to give you hope and a future'"* (Jeremiah 29:11 NIV).

Religion teaches that it is not Christ-like to seek advancement. However, nothing is more supportive of Christ's teachings than taking the good news of salvation to the lost; that is His whole purpose for elevating you! An elevated life is His 'Madison Avenue' advertising campaign for drawing people into the Kingdom.

Knowing that your prosperous future is the plan God uses to draw others to Him, you can joyfully stride into that future anticipating the new heights you are sure to encounter. That makes me want to race toward the future He has planned for me! But, hold on . . . we have so much more to discover!

NO SHORTCUTS

M ost often, what prevents us from reaching new heights is not enemy interference, as many assert. It is failing to assimilate a strategy that promotes what God has designed. By failing to embrace God's strategy, we actually begin opposing His plan.

Many of us have computerized GPS instruments in our cars or 'smart' phones that can quickly formulate a route to take us from Point A to Point B. These clever devices can even calculate traffic flow and detours that you may encounter on the trip.

As long as you follow the route on the GPS screen, you will arrive at the planned destination. What does not work so well is failing to look at the route—even though it is right there on your dashboard. Worse yet is thinking, "I believe I know a shortcut"—even though you have never been there before and have no clue about landmarks along the way.

Now you are opposing the GPS. This strategy prevents you from reaching your destination. In fact, by failing to embrace the GPS' strategy, you will be lost, confused, and force the instrument to 'recalculate' your position.

When we ignore or oppose God's strategy by thinking our way will work better, we will never reach the destination He planned for us. That is what happened to the children of Israel after leaving Egypt.

When God delivered the Israelites from Egyptian bondage, they began traveling toward their Promised Land, but few of them lived to possess it. Because they failed to trust and implement God's plan, they did not reach their destination. In fact, by diligently *opposing* God's plan, they had to recalculate and wander in the desert for 40 years. Their children entered, but none of the long caravan following Moses ever made it.

GOD'S GPS

The enemy's success lies not in demolishing your future (he does not have one), but in causing you to doubt or fail to execute God's strategy for your life. He wants you to ignore God's GPS—His Word and the guidance of the Holy Spirit—and trust your own sense of direction.

While the devil cannot prevent you from attaining your final destination of eternity with the Father, he loves to keep you recalculating and stuck at base camp the rest of your life.

The Holy Spirit is the surest Guide to your destination. Before taking a step out of base camp, surrender completely to His strategy to take you to the top.

MIRROR, MIRROR

We should be keenly aware of the necessary prophetic forces working in our lives that will expedite our trip to the top. Apart from God's Word and the influence of the Holy Spirit, the most significant of these forces is the company we keep.

According to an old saying, friends are like mirrors; you can see yourself by looking at them. That is well and good if the friends you have chosen reflect a good image. But like the mirrors in a carnival fun house, ill-chosen friends can reflect an absurd distortion with no similarity to the image of God in which you were created.

How you see yourself has a dominant impact on your destiny, because your thoughts and actions are based on your self-image.

The friends you choose shape how you see yourself; how you see yourself has a dominant impact on your destiny, because your thoughts and actions are based on your self-image.

JUST LIKE MAMA MADE

Where I'm from in South Louisiana, mothers teach their daughters to make gumbo "just like Mama made." You see, there is more to a good gumbo roux than mixing oil and flour. Seasoning secrets and heating temperatures are passed from grandmother to mother to daughter, and from family to family.

Cajun cooks know that it takes flour, oil, and heat to make a roux. That is a Southern Louisiana universal truth. But how each family applies that truth—the ratio of flour to oil and the level and endurance of the heat—is what makes a unique roux.

So how does making gumbo relate to your destiny? If you live in the Atchafalaya Basin, it could mean a lot; but there is still a very important principle to grasp. Just like a daughter instinctively mixes and heats flour and oil at the same temperature and amount of time as her mother and grandmother, most of us replicate thoughts and behaviors of those with whom we have spent the most time.

Put another way: we make choices and decisions based on the truth we have been exposed to and how we apply that truth in day-to-day living. It has only been since our conversion that we live according to the truth of Jeremiah 29:11, "God has a good and prosperous plan for us." If blessed to associate with those who also know this truth and readily pursue God's plans with excitement and enthusiasm, chances are we will do the same.

However, if our closest associates are those who do not courageously anticipate a future filled with hope—even though exposed to this truth—we will have a much harder time personally applying this truth.

STRATEGICALLY EXPAND YOUR REPERTOIRE

Purposefully and thoughtfully choosing friends and associates has tremendous impact on how your journey ends. Others can expose you to anointings that were not previously part of your repertoire. Therefore, it is possible, through strategic associations and relationships with those at a higher level, to elevate your life.

According to Scripture, strategic relationships can actually transform you into a different person. In 1 Samuel, the prophet gives these instructions to King Saul:

> *"After that you will go to Gilbeah of God, where there is a Philistine outpost. As you approach the town, you will meet a procession of prophets*

> *coming down from the high places...The spirit
> of the Lord will come powerfully upon you, and
> you will prophesy with them; and **you will
> be changed into a different person**"*
> (1 Samuel 10:5-6 NIV).

Saul was *"changed into a different person"* by intentionally creating a relationship with a group of people *"coming down from the high (elevated) places."*

The word 'Gilbeah' means *hill* or *high place*. After meeting a group of prophets who had come from the elevated place of God, Saul received an impartation of anointing that was not in his original DNA. The Spirit of the Lord caused him to function in a prophetical gift he had never experienced before that encounter. Consequently, by strategically connecting with this group, his life was elevated.

NATURE ABHORS A VACUUM

When you connect with a higher level of anointing, as did Saul and the prophets from Gilbeah, the Spiritual Law of Transference creates a demand upon that anointing. Scientists understand this law of physics: nature abhors a vacuum, or a level of high pressure always flows into a level of low pressure.

This is what happened to the woman with the issue of blood (Mark 5:25-31). Because she believed that touching the hem of Jesus' garment would make her whole, the vacuum within her placed a demand upon His anointing—and it happened! This truth, both natural and spiritual, made her well. When His powerful anointing passed into the vacuum within her, she then had the same *authority* over the illness that Jesus had.

Jesus has supreme authority over every spiritual dimension. This is why the most important relationship to pursue is with Him. Elevation will manifest as you learn how to exercise His authority in all dimensions and to make demands on the anointings in Him.

The purpose of this book is to discuss spiritual dimensions and how to exercise true authority in each of them. Understanding the first four principles is essential to experiencing higher altitudes in Christ. As you continue the ascent, frequently remind yourself:

1. God has *good* plans for me (and it is okay to believe that).

2. God's GPS is smarter than I am (so I won't have to recalculate).

3. The company I keep and the gumbo I make (i.e., the truth I'm exposed to and how I apply that truth) are dominant forces in determining my destiny.

4. Strategic associations can transform me into a different person (recall what happened when I met Jesus!).

Chapter 2

YOU CAN GET THERE FROM HERE

No one sprints to the top of Mount Everest. Regardless of the many months of training and preparation, once on the mountain, climbers must make each step deliberate and calculated. You must make frequent stops along the way for the body to acclimate to successively higher elevations.

Everest expeditions begin by flying from Kathmandu, Nepal into the most dangerous airport in the world, Tenzing-Hillary Airport at Lukla. This short, steep airstrip, coupled with unpredictable, violent weather, often results in fatal crashes[3]. From Lukla, it's a two-day hike to the village of Namche Bazaar, the climbers' first altitude acclimation stop.

Mountaineers must then trek to Everest Base Camp just south of the Khumbu Icefall, one of the most dangerous areas on the mountain. After several days of final preparations and

---

[3] http://en.wikipedia.org/wiki/Lukla

allowing their bodies to adapt, they set out for the next four progressively higher base camps toward the summit.

The final respite before the ultimate push along the Southern Col to the 28,700-foot peak is known as "The Balcony"—or as many say, the "death zone."

At The Balcony, climbers face a succession of formidable rock steps that force them to walk through waist-deep snow, presenting a serious threat of avalanche. At this elevation of about 26,000 feet, severe altitude sickness can be fatal.

Just as Everest mountaineers meticulously plan and measure their ascent, this elevation requires conscientious thought and action, the key word being 'action.' You can stand outside your tent (or sit on a church pew) all your life, admiring the magnificent peaks and daydreaming about the next view; but until you determine to put one foot in front of the other and proceed with a planned strategy, you'll be going nowhere in the Kingdom.

LEAVING LUKLA

The seven steps below are your jumping-off point. Think of them as your spiritual Lukla where the trek actually begins. With each serving an indispensable purpose, study them carefully. Remember, there are no shortcuts up that mountain!

1. *Elevate your life by elevating your God.*

The process of an elevated life begins with elevating our God. In this first step of the expedition you must unequivocally decide who and what is 'Number 1' in your life. Just a hint, God does not do very well as Number 2.

We tend to elevate many things above God. That first spot may be a job, finances, or family. Another word for this is *idolatry*. An idol can be anything that you give your time, talents, and thoughts to more than to God.

God never blesses idolatry. Quite the contrary, He commands us to move as quickly as possible from any trace of this sin. *"Therefore, my dearly beloved, shun (keep clear away from, avoid by flight if need be) any sort of idolatry (of loving or venerating anything more than God)"* (1 Corinthians 10:14 AMP).

Elevating your job, money, or family above God will never release His divine transference for reaching the next level. The anointing and gifting required for the next level can only flow into our lives from God's abundance.

2. ***Elevate God by elevating His Kingdom.***

Matthew 6:33 says, *"But seek ye **first** the Kingdom of God and His righteousness and all these things shall be added to you."* To elevate God's Kingdom, priority must be given to what is important to Him. This is how to position yourself for supernatural elevation.

While cars can quickly transport you to many places, one thing a car cannot do is fly—at least not for any distance that matters or ends well. To reach a higher elevation requires an airplane.

The Boeing Airbus A380-800 is the largest passenger airliner in the world. With a 5,145 square foot cabin, it can transport over 800 people, plus cargo. So, if a vehicle is parked in the cargo section and the plane takes off, the car is now flying.

In this new position, the restrictions of aerodynamics, gravity, and geography no longer apply to the car. Since God's Word says that we are *in* Christ, because of our position *in* Him, we have abilities that otherwise could never be attained.

> When we are *in* Christ, He takes us places we could never dream of going on our own.

Just like the car traveling in the Airbus cargo section, when we are *in* Christ, He takes us places we could never dream of going on our own.

Jesus said that His church could do even greater things than the first disciples. While nothing can be accomplished in our own power, when we position ourselves in the A380 known as "Jesus and His Kingdom," we can do what He did—and more!

3. *Elevate the Kingdom by elevating His Word.*

Elevating God's Word means we give it authority over our life by allowing it the final say in all we think or do. It also means giving His Word the honor and acclaim that God Himself gives it: *"For you have magnified your word above all your name"* (Psalm 138:2 NKJV).

Many Christians want to pick-and-choose what they will accept from God's Word. They mix a little Genesis here, a verse from the Psalms there, a touch of the Gospels, a pinch of Acts, and a few lines from the Pauline epistles. That becomes their boarding pass for the Airbus 380, which is Christ. Believe me, they will never even make it through security!

They are unsure if *all* of God's Word applies in our *modern* world. Yet, these same people claim to love the name of Jesus above every name and venerate the many names of Jehovah. But God said that His Word is to be magnified even *above* His name!

To experience God's ultimate, supernatural elevation, we must accept the authority of His Word without question or hesitation. Stop vacillating! Determine to submit to and revere the *entire* Word of God. To elevate God's Kingdom, we must elevate what matters to Him, and His Word—**all** of it—matters to Him.

4. *Elevate God's Word by elevating your commitment.*

To fly on a commercial airline, you must buy a ticket, get a boarding pass, and go to your seat. But if you refuse to fasten your seatbelt or turn off your cell phone when it's time for takeoff, you'll be escorted off the plane. Passengers who fail to obey the safety precautions cannot fly on that airline.

God's Word contains His Kingdom principles; you can accept salvation, be baptized in water and the Holy Spirit, and become a church member. But if you fail to abide by Kingdom principles found in His Word, you will be grounded. You are not going anywhere in Jesus.

In the last few decades, an insidious transformation has taken place in the church. Christians have come to accept a culture that does not reflect a commitment to the principles of God's Word. Instead, we have settled for a watered-down culture of activity without anointing, growth without glory, ministry without mission, purpose without prayer, and service without sacrifice.

This culture of wishy-washy, half-hearted Christianity has grounded the church far too long. That version of Christianity does not position the church *in* Christ, ready for takeoff; it only positions us to sit on a church pew on Sunday mornings.

Psalm 138:1 says we are to praise God with our *"whole heart,"* and 99.9 per cent is not the 'whole.' Pushing forward to dizzying heights in God's plans will require going all-out for the Kingdom.

5. *Elevate your commitment by elevating the mission.*

Three of the gospels poignantly relate a story of what happens when the church's mission is elevated. Christ's mission on earth was to die for the salvation of the world. That was His assignment.

The crowds that thronged Jesus, longing to see another sign or miracle, were clueless about His purpose.

15

If His disciples were aware at all, they soundly rejected the plan. Only Mary of Bethany with her alabaster flask of perfume chose to sacrificially align herself with His mission.

While Jesus was the guest at a Pharisee's home, Mary knelt before Him, openly weeping. As her tears moistened His feet, she dried them with her hair and then leaned forward to kiss them. Then Mary broke an expensive flask of perfume and poured it over Jesus' feet.

Jesus understood the significance of what she had done. When His disciples complained about her 'wasteful' act (a year's wages), Jesus reprimanded them:

> *"When she poured this perfume on my body, she did it to prepare me for burial"* (Matthew 26:12 NIV).

Whether she fully understood or not, at that pivotal moment, Mary was assisting the fulfillment of Jesus' assignment by preparing His body for the burial that would soon follow. She was giving her whole heart to further Christ's mission.

God elevates those who are devoted to what matters to Him.

Then Jesus declared for generations to come the impact of Mary's loving act:

> *"Truly I tell you, wherever this gospel is preached throughout the world, what she has done will also be told, in memory of her"* (Matthew 26:13 NIV).

And here we are, over two thousand years later, still talking about it.

God elevates those who are devoted to what matters to Him. His mission—reaching the lost and transforming their lives—matters to Him. Pour your life into what matters to Him, and enjoy the view on your way to the top.

6. *Elevate the mission by elevating your church.*

An ever-growing trend in the United States is for folks to 'do their own thing.' They will have 'church' (if they attend at all) in someone's back yard or a kitchen table, rather than attending a local assembly.

These well-meaning Christians believe in the church's mission to preach the gospel to all the world, yet they won't unite with a local congregation to assist a single mom's child across the street with an after-school program or deliver a basket of food once a month. They are all for building God's Kingdom globally, . . . but not locally.

Having a family altar is great, but it does not replace corporate fellowship. Since the Kingdom is composed of local churches all over the world, you cannot build the Kingdom without building the local church.

Believers have abandoned the mission of the church, which connects this nameless mass of people who meet around the globe on Sundays. The very predictable result of this withdrawal is that the 'mission' is never accomplished.

There is no room for different interpretations of God's Word on this subject. He did not say, "Hang out wherever you feel like worshiping." Instead, He very specifically told believers where to attend:

> *"Arise and go **up** to Bethel, and settle there and build an altar there to God"* (Genesis 35:1 NIV).

The word *Bethel* means 'house of God.' Put simply, this scripture instructs us to go to a local church, settle in, and then carve a place of worship and service in that congregation.

Nowhere in Scripture has this instruction been changed or canceled. Rather, it has been continually echoed and repeated:

- *"Come now, and let us reason **together**,"* (Isaiah 1:18 NKJV).

- *"Let us exalt His name **together**,"* (Psalm 34:3 NKJV).

- *"Not forsaking the assembling of ourselves **together**, as is the manner of some,"* (Hebrews 10:25 NKJV).

It seems very clear that God intends our service and worship to be communal. Still, many reject this condition, abandon the journey, and never fulfill the elevated destiny God planned for them.

Be careful not to fall into the trap of justifying yourself by accusing the church of being filled with hypocrites with inflated egos who only want your money. While that may be true in some congregations, it could be true of any group of people.

Yes, there are unscrupulous, hypocritical officers in every police force, but when someone is breaking into your home, you will still dial 9-1-1. Many politicians have huge egos, but on Election Day, we will vote for the best possible candidate to govern our community. Some doctors are only interested in your money, but that does not prevent you from making an appointment if symptoms of cancer appear.

Expect the house of God to be situated in an elevated location, because transformation occurs at the high places. When Saul met a group of prophets returning from the high place of worship, God transformed him into a different person.

To experience real elevation, go *up* to your local house of worship, join fellow believers in service, and let God transform you into the image of Himself you were created to be.

7. *Elevate your church by elevating your mission.*

God made you in His image for a reason. You are here on a mission. *Your* mission and *the* mission are distinct, yet closely related. By fulfilling *your* mission within a local church, *the* mission will be accomplished.

At the core of the local church are people who have been harmoniously joined together to pursue individual missions. To elevate your church, elevate your mission within that local congregation.

Realizing and fulfilling your specific purpose reveals whether you are truly God's child. Supernatural elevation occurs when you discern your specific mission, then passionately involve your hands and feet in corporate service to our heavenly Father.

GOD'S ENTOURAGE

Wherever they travel, rock stars and movie icons have their own entourage. Their star-struck followers have no talent, good looks, or money; but by closely associating with the VIP, they enjoy a certain degree of elevated earthly status.

The same is true, on an infinitely superior scale, for those in God's entourage. When you begin to elevate God with these seven steps, in the process He will elevate you. Because of this association, He takes you along for the ride. Your elevated life becomes a flashing neon sign, which will guide lost souls to the Father.

Chapter 3

ROPES AND LADDERS

As Everest mountaineers acclimate to the altitude at EBC, their porters and guides are busy erecting ladder and rope systems to navigate through the very dangerous Khumbu Icefall. Situated at the head of the Khumbu Glacier (the world's largest glacier), this icefall is located just above EBC and marks the beginning of the journey.

Typical guides for Everest excursions are Sherpa, Nepali natives, famous for their extraordinary climbing ability and stamina in extreme heights. Some speculate their abilities are the result of genetic adaptations from living in high altitudes. Their physical ability and understanding of the mountain's terrain render them indispensable to expeditions.

The rope and ladder climbing system created by the Sherpa guides helps climbers navigate through this very dangerous area. The Khumbu Glacier moves approximately three to four feet per day, enough for large crevasses to quickly form beneath a climber's feet or for ice towers to crumble with no warning. Loss of life is common here.

Novice climbers waiting in the safety of EBC do not fully understand the importance of the climbing system constructed in advance by their Sherpa guides, but you had better believe, once their feet hit the slippery slopes of the icefall, they quickly acquire a profound appreciation for their guides' strategic structure.

GOD'S STRATEGIC STRUCTURE

The most basic definition of the word 'strategy' is: something done in advance to achieve a desired future result. The desired result is God's promise for a good future and elevated destiny. His strategy is to expedite the manifestation of His promises while you exercise your authority in twelve consecutive spiritual dimensions. In sequential order, those twelve dimensions are:

1. Authority over Self
2. Authority in a Family Structure
3. Authority over Secular Affairs
4. Authority in a Ministry Structure
5. Authority over Demonic Systems
6. Authority over Resources
7. Authority over Seasons
8. Authority over Communities
9. Authority over Regions
10. Authority to Heal
11. Authority over Dimensions
12. Authority *with God* over Nature

Spiritual authority is the important, yet missing component in our efforts to establish God's Kingdom in the earth and fulfill His will for our lives. It is also one of the most misunderstood principles in the church today.

IF YOU HAVE TO TELL FOLKS
YOU'RE THE BOSS...

To better understand what spiritual authority is, let's clear up what it is **not**. Spiritual authority is **not** some religious bigwig strutting about, touting himself as 'God's man of power for the hour.' It's not about giving yourself an important sounding title or demanding approval from a bullied congregation. Much harm has been done by those claiming to have or attempting to exercise spiritual authority where they have none. (More on this later.)

Like the old saying, *if you have to tell folks you are the boss, you're not*. Having a title does not mean you have achieved a commensurate level of spiritual authority.

Neither is spiritual authority synonymous with spiritual power. Power and authority are two distinct entities. As Jesus pointed out, we need *both* to fulfill God's work on the earth:

> *"When Jesus called the twelve together, He gave them power **and** authority to drive out all demons and to cure diseases, and He sent them out to proclaim the kingdom of God and to heal the sick"* (Luke 9:1-2 NIV).

The church's problem is not a lack of power. Every believer who has been baptized in the Holy Spirit has been entrusted with the same power that spoke the world into existence and raised Christ from the grave:

> *"Now to Him who is able to do exceedingly abundantly above all that we ask or think,* **according to the power that works in us"** (Ephesians 3:20 NKJV).

Through the baptism of the Holy Spirit, we become spiritual nuclear reactors. We achieve elevation not by procuring more power, but by attaining more authority. The sad reality is most believers never experience the supernatural breakthrough that accompanies these advanced dimensions because they fail to exercise their God-given spiritual authority.

There are seven reasons for this failure:

1. **Believers do not understand the meaning of spiritual authority.**

    You cannot inhabit a level of spiritual authority that you do not know exists. When speaking of the lost, Paul said it like this:

    > *"How then shall they call on Him in whom they have not believed? And how shall they believe in Him of whom they have not heard? And how shall they hear without a preacher?"* (Romans 10:14 KJV).

Put another way: You do not know that you don't know what you don't know.

2. Believers fail to submit to spiritual authority.

Submitting to spiritual authority does not mean cowering to the whims of a church leader on a power trip. Rather, it is giving honor where honor is due (Romans 13:7) and willingly deferring to those recognized to be at a higher level of authority.

The story of the centurion in Matthew 8:5-13 most aptly illustrates the importance of recognizing and submitting to spiritual authority. Recognizing that Jesus' authority over illness flowed from His submission to *the* Authority, the centurion affirmed that Jesus only had to send a word and his servant would be healed.

"For I also am a man under authority, having soldiers under me. And I say to this one 'Go,' and he goes; and to another 'Come,' and he comes," (Matthew 8:9 NKJV).

Jesus unconditionally and unequivocally submitted to the will of the Father. Consequently, He could operate in a dimension where a mere spoken word could heal all manner of sickness or even raise the dead.

"Then Jesus said to the centurion, 'Go your way; and as you have believed, so let it be done for you.' And his servant was healed that same hour" (Matthew 8:13 NKJV).

3. **Believers are not spiritually mature.**

If you are a child of God and heir to His
Kingdom, you automatically have the right name and
DNA. That is all the power you need! However, a father
who owns a business would never entrust his company
to an immature son or daughter who would rather spend
money on bubble gum than paying bills.

> *"As long as an heir is under age, he is no
> more than a slave, although he owns the
> whole estate. The heir is subject to guardians
> and trustees until the time set by his father"*
> (Galatians 4:1-2 NIV).

Until we are spiritually mature, we are *"no more
than a slave,"* regardless of our birthright privileges.

It is imperative that we grow to spiritual maturity
by increasing our understanding of God's ways. We must
be able to determine what is happening, as well as the
reason for it.

> *"Consider it pure joy, my brothers and sisters,
> whenever you face trials of many kinds,
> because you know that the testing of your
> faith produces perseverance. Let perseverance
> finish its work so that you may be **mature**
> and complete, not lacking anything"*
> (James 1:2-4 NIV).

4. **Believers are not faithful stewards.**

Statistics show that the average church-going Christian gives nine-tenths of one percent of their income, which is not even tithing on the tithe! By definition, a tithe is ten percent. Not only do many not tithe, they will not even give God a 'tip!'

With such meager giving, it is no wonder the church is so ineffective in reaching the lost, the sick, and the hurting. There is no money! But more importantly, because of their poor stewardship habits, Christians have *no authority* to take dominion over the kingdom of darkness.

Most disturbing about these statistics is that believers are content to have no authority to tackle big issues—cancer, drug addiction, divorce—until it is *their* cancer, drug addiction or divorce! They are satisfied to give their nine-tenths of one percent and remain spiritually anemic until *they* need supernatural power to pry their child from the hideous grasp of drug addiction or restore a spouse from the black abyss of infidelity.

The devil wants Christians to continue believing stewardship is 'not New Testament' or only helps the *fat cats* to grow fatter. He knows that when we awaken to the truth that stewardship empowers us with authority to take control of his domain, he is in serious trouble! If we forcefully tell him to go away, he has no choice but to comply.

In the parable of the talents (Luke 19:12-27), Jesus directly relates the right to legitimately exercise spiritual authority to faithful stewards. In this allegory, being faithful in a 'very little' caused the servant to be promoted and have authority over entire cities!

God will not entrust the riches of spiritual authority to those who cannot be trusted with mammon that has no lasting value. Until we can prove ourselves trustworthy, the church will never possess authority for instant healing of disease or casting out demons in drug-infested inner cities.

5. **Believers do not hunger for spiritual authority.**

I was taught to believe that fasting was some sort of spiritual arm-twisting Christians engaged in when they wanted something special from God. Of course, that is not true. Everything He wanted to release into our lives has already been spoken in the heavenly realms.

> Fasting empties you of self so you can hunger for the things of God.

Fasting is a powerful spiritual discipline that serves many purposes, one of which breaks the stronghold of the physical world and increases spiritual hunger. Fasting empties you of self so you can hunger for the things of God.

No doubt, Jesus' disciples wielded a certain spiritual authority. Yet, when they were asked to cast out a demon from a possessed child, they were powerless to do so (Mark 9:14-29). However, when Jesus spoke to the demon, it immediately left.

This prompted the disciples' question: *"'Why could we not cast it out?' So He said to them, 'This kind can come out by nothing but prayer and fasting',"* (Mark 9:28-29 NKJV). Although they had achieved a certain level of spiritual authority, there were higher levels for them to seek. To reach those levels, they had to hunger for them.

There is an old saying, "A hungry man has no manners." A friend of mine witnessed this one day in the cafeteria of a large, public safety-net hospital. When a compassionate person purchased a lunch for a homeless man, he began using his hands to cram the meatloaf and potatoes into his mouth. Although it was quite a spectacle to those nearby, the hungry man paid no attention.

That is what the church needs: a hunger that drives us to abandon our Sunday morning manners and gorge ourselves on His Word and presence until our famished spirits are absorbed with His life-giving Spirit.

6. **Believers have weak faith.**

Nothing in nature will grow without food. Animal life, plant life, microscopic life—all life forms need nourishment. The specific type of nourishment depends on the life form.

The spirit is fed by reading God's Word and serving Him. Jesus told His disciples, *"My food is to do the will of Him who sent Me, and to finish His work,"* (John 4:34 NIV). When you feed your spirit, your faith becomes strong.

"So then faith comes by hearing, and hearing by the word of God," (Romans 10:17 NKJV). To function in spiritual authority, you must hear a nourishing Word from God that strengthens your faith.

This is why church attendance is essential. Faith will not grow unless it is fed, and it is fed by *"assembling together"* to worship, serve, and hear a faith-producing, faith-strengthening Word from God.

7. **Believers are content with the status quo.**

For too long, the church has succumbed to a climate God never intended for us to inhabit. Having been created in His image and saturated with His resurrection power, we continue to think according to our human weaknesses and tolerate spiritual anemia, rather than our newfound strength.

Change is difficult. We avoid it because we know it causes discomfort. A word of warning: as you move into higher elevations, expect to encounter some serious discomfort. When it comes, remember to make adjustments for your new altitude.

Your new altitude may become so unbearable, you will consider returning to a lower elevation. Don't do it! Remember the complaining Israelites? They even longed for the brutal taskmasters rather than the discomforts of change.

"All the Israelites grumbled against Moses and Aaron…'If only we had died in Egypt or in this wilderness! Why is the Lord bringing us to this land only to let us die by the sword? Wouldn't it be better for us to go back to Egypt?'…And they said to each other 'We should choose a leader and go back to Egypt'" (Numbers 14:2-4 NIV).

Egypt was a miserable experience; but returning to their status quo seemed more desirable than crossing the Jordan River to an unknown Promised Land.

That is where many believers reside. Sitting in their pew at base camp, all they can see are the dangers of the Khumbu Icefall. They would rather wait there for Jesus' return than brave the unknowns of the next level.

The good news is, once your feet hit the ice, you will discover God has already devised a strategy to transport you across the unfamiliar landscape of the new heights. By discerning His marvelous network of 'ropes and ladders,' you can climb with confidence to the next elevation, knowing your Guide has gone before you.

Chapter 4

WARNING:
SLIPPERY SLOPE AHEAD

As mentioned before, crossing the Khumbu Icefall is extremely dangerous because of the constantly shifting glacier. Khumbu Glacier descends Mount Everest toward Base Camp at about three to four feet per day. At this rate, towers of ice as large as a 12-story building can break free and fall without warning. Avalanches and falling ice blocks are common. Snow bridges are likely to form, concealing deadly crevasses beneath.

At this first stage of an Everest climb, many either turn back or lose their lives. Wise, skilled navigators are required to reach Camp 1, just above the top of the icefall.

True spiritual authority is the church's key missing component to establish God's Kingdom on earth. A thorough understanding of this essential element is imperative. So, do not lose your footing on this slippery slope at the very outset of your trip to the top.

THE PUZZLING ELEMENT OF
SPIRITUAL AUTHORITY

M any think they know what spiritual authority is, but much of our reference frame is contorted. The models to which we have been exposed usually deal with, "Who's the boss?"

Real spiritual authority is **not** domineering. Its basis is altogether different, which has puzzled religious leaders for centuries.

> *"They arrived again in Jerusalem, and while Jesus*
> *was walking in the temple courts, the chief priests,*
> *the teachers of the law, and the elders came to him.*
> *'By what **authority** are you doing these things?'*
> *they asked. 'And who gave you **authority** to do*
> *this?'"* (Mark 11:27-28 NIV).

The 'things' Jesus was questioned about were the three dimensions of spiritual authority He had demonstrated in the last few days:

- **Authority over resources:** Two disciples were told to bring a colt upon which no one had ridden and to secure it with these words: "The Lord needs it" (Mark 11:1-3). Amazingly, the owner gave it to the disciples because of Jesus' authority over resources. In our day, the cost of a donkey would be comparable to a new car.

- **Authority over seasons:** Jesus cursed a fig tree that failed to produce fruit for Him—even though it was not the time of figs—and it instantly died (Mark 11:12-14). While that may seem unfair, it was because the tree was out of alignment with spiritual authority.

- **Authority over demonic and religious systems** (which are closely linked): Jesus plaited a cord of whips and drove the moneychangers out of the Temple (Mark 11:15-17).

It is your voice— not your position, that determines your spiritual authority.

Since the Temple money-changers far outnumbered Jesus, they could have refused to listen. The fact that they obeyed was so unnerving to those with superior titles, they questioned the source of Jesus' authority (Mark 11:27-28). Why had these merchants submitted to the authority of Jesus' spoken words? It is your voice—not your position, that determines your spiritual authority.

UNDERSTANDING THE NATURAL COMES FIRST

Examining secular authority will more clearly explain the many dimensions of spiritual authority. Learning the natural always helps to discern the spiritual (1 Corinthians 15:46).

For example, we know that when a natural seed of corn falls to the ground and dies, it will sprout into a stalk of corn with incalculable future generations. Because Jesus used a familiar 'resurrection' example from the realm of nature, we can more readily understand how His death, burial, and resurrection could purchase our salvation and eternal life. It is much easier to understand the spiritual if we first understand the natural.

Of the twelve types of secular authority, elements of all but one can be found in the dimensions of spiritual authority.

1. **Functional authority** is the authority we give one another to help us function properly; for example, authority in the home of parents over children.

2. **Persuasive authority** is granted to the person who inspires others to embrace their leadership; for example, one person can persuade others to take a certain route to the football game to avoid heavy traffic.

3. **Legislated authority** is established by our governmental system. We obey this authority because the law requires it; to disobey results in unpleasant consequences.

4. **Delegated authority** is passed from one person to another. If the boss promotes you to oversee a particular assignment in the company, you are given delegated authority to accomplish the task.

5. **Hierarchical authority** is the authority an employer exerts because of their title in the organization.

6. **Technical authority** is granted where a specific expertise is required. We submit to the authority of a pilot or surgeon because of their technical certification.

7. **Negotiated authority** is granted after parameters and guidelines have been discussed. When a husband and wife both have jobs outside the home, an agreement will be reached to handle household responsibilities.

8. **Traditional authority** is seen in societies where roles and responsibilities are assigned according to cultural practice.

9. **Charismatic authority** is granted to one who is highly regarded. Martin Luther King, Jr. and Jim Jones both exercised charismatic authority, but with totally opposite results.

10. **Relational authority** is given to close friends or family. Because this authority directly and profoundly affects the fulfillment of your destiny, it could well be the most important type of secular authority.

11. **Natural authority** is the pre-existing legislative authority recognized as legitimate. It is a society's 'self-evident' authority to stand for equality and fair treatment of all in that society.

12. **Coercive authority** is the one type that **has no correlation to the spiritual.** Imposed upon others by force, this is the authority wielded by school bullies or dictators. Surprisingly, this type is the first that comes to mind when discussing spiritual authority. Beware! Those who stumble into the perilous clefts of this slippery slope will fail to achieve the elevation God intended!

Spiritual authority, as God intends for us to employ, is the lawful right to:

- Make decisions and implement strategies that affect our lives and His Kingdom and to fulfill the church's mission;

- Call forth and utilize the resources of heaven and earth to fund the Kingdom and our destiny;

- Address and remove resistance for the advancement of Kingdom purposes and our destinies.

PAUL'S GREATEST ACT OF SPIRITUAL AUTHORITY

One of the best examples of exercising true spiritual authority is the apostle Paul. Everywhere he went, he spoke with authority to demons and disease—and they obeyed. But even these powerful acts were not his best representations.

Paul's spiritual authority was best revealed from the opposition he faced at Antioch. This is where he *submitted* to converts' requests to have the church elders at Jerusalem judge whether his teaching about Gentile circumcision was correct (Acts 15).

Having authored more than half of the New Testament, experienced a personal revelation from the risen Lord, beaten, imprisoned, and shipwrecked for the sake of the gospel, Paul responded in true servanthood to the Gentile converts' requests, then submitted to the authority of the Jewish council at Jerusalem.

In the natural, Paul had every right to counter, "Because I said so, that's why!" But it never happened because he was *a man under authority.*

True spiritual authority does not 'lord' over someone else. It is based on the servanthood and submission portrayed in Christ's ministry. The very source of Jesus' authority baffled the religious leaders who questioned Him. Because of the sharp contrast between the coercive authority they exerted and understood, they could not comprehend Christ's form of jurisdiction.

Comprehending the true meaning of spiritual authority is like strapping on your spiritual crampons, a spiked iron plate worn on a climber's boots to prevent slipping. You can now sure-footedly traverse the icy climb ahead. The remainder of this book will delve into dimensions of spiritual authority and how to master them. Bring along those things with which you are now equipped. And remember, no running!

Chapter 5

MADE FOR MORE!

B ecause of two potentially fatal altitude sicknesses, HACE (high altitude cerebral edema) and HAPE (high altitude pulmonary edema), wise climbers are extremely cautious about ascending too quickly. Only after their bodies have acclimated to their current altitude will they very slowly ascend Everest.

Similarly, each dimension of spiritual authority must be mastered before pressing toward the next. Some form of 'altitude sickness' discussed in the last chapter may also be expected. Just as continual hurricane force winds are experienced at certain times of the year on Everest's pinnacle, you will know you're headed in the right direction when storm winds begin to blow.

REAL KINGDOM LIVING

S alvation is not the climax of your spiritual quest. While Sunday morning pew warming seems to be the calling of many, these folks have not even filled their backpacks! They have no idea of the gorgeous panoramas just beyond base camp, and you can bet they never attract anyone to the Kingdom.

> **Real Kingdom living is a continual advancement to new heights by attaining new levels of spiritual authority.**

Real Kingdom living is a perpetual adventure. It is a continual advancement to new heights by attaining new levels of spiritual authority. Salvation is merely the first landmark on the mountain.

Jesus promised,

"My Father's house has many rooms; if that were not so, would I have told you that I am going there to prepare a place for you?" (John 14:2 NIV).

The word *rooms* in this familiar scripture literally means 'places to stay' in the Kingdom's varied dimensions. Some choose to remain in salvation base camp, while others strap on their crampons and boldly pursue higher altitudes.

To move from one *place* to another requires the proper key:

"I will give you the keys of the kingdom of heaven; whatever you bind on earth will be bound in heaven, and whatever you loose on earth will be loosed in heaven" (Matthew 16:19 NIV).

This is one of those scriptures that urges me to challenge tradition. For decades, religion has taught that salvation requires multiple keys, which is totally wrong! Jesus said, *"I am **the** door. If anyone enters by Me, he will be saved"* (John 10:9 NKJV).

Multiple keys are not required to open a single door! Jesus Christ is the only door that allows entrance to the Kingdom. However, once inside, multiple keys are necessary to open the *many rooms,* or spiritual dimensions that await us.

The translation of the word 'whatever' literally means: *if,* or *in case.* So, to paraphrase:

> *"I give you the keys of the kingdom of heaven, so if, or in case, you have the keys, you can bind or loose the thing for which you have the key."*

Each dimension has its own key that Jesus must give us. To unlock and inhabit higher levels of spiritual authority will require replacing religious rule with Holy Spirit revelation.

YOU HAVE AN ENEMY!

One problem in exercising spiritual authority is accepting the fact that an enemy is plotting to bypass everything God wants to do in your life. Make no mistake, a malicious enemy is plotting to do you harm!

He is much like the balding man in the post office who was methodically placing 'Love' stamps on bright pink envelopes covered with hearts. A customer standing nearby became so curious, he asked about the stamps and envelopes. The man replied, "I'm sending out a thousand 'I Love You' cards signed, 'Guess who?'"

"But, why?" asked the by-stander.

"I'm a divorce attorney."

GIVE CREDIT WHERE CREDIT IS DUE

In the parable of the tares, Jesus confirmed that we have an enemy whose goal is to destroy us:

> *"The kingdom of heaven is like a man who sowed good seed in his field; but while men slept, his enemy came and sowed tares among the wheat and went his way. But when the grain had sprouted and produced a crop, then the tares also appeared. So the servants of the owner came and said to him, 'Sir, did you not sow good seed in your field? How then does it have tares?' He said to them, 'An enemy has done this'"* (Matthew 13:24-28 NKJV).

When bad things happen, people often look in the wrong direction to place the blame. "Why did God do this?" they say. The only thing the enemy likes better than sowing evil is to persuade people to blame God for His cruelty.

Since the enemy's goal is to prevent you from enjoying the prosperity God planned for you, elevation will require the exercise of spiritual authority over your future.

THE QUAGMIRE OF TRADITION AND RELIGION

Coupled with the enemy's aggressive opposition, tradition and religion are also conspiring to prevent the fulfillment of your destiny. While tradition causes you to reject new methods or ideas, religion prevents you from believing that God can empower you to function in spiritual authority.

Back in the 18th century, Church of England cleric John Wesley rejected the tradition that a sermon could only be preached from a church pulpit on Sunday mornings. His 'open air' services for the masses were the genesis of what we know as the Methodist church.[4]

Two hundred years earlier, German priest Martin Luther sparked the Reformation by publicly rejecting the teachings of the Catholic Church. Because he opened his mind to God's Word sans religious dogma, he was excommunicated, dubbed an outlaw, and founded the Protestant faith.[5]

Once Wesley and Luther could no longer tolerate tradition and religion or accept the status quo, they pressed upward to the next level. The result was countless souls coming to know *"the incomparable riches of [God's] grace, expressed in His kindness to us in Christ Jesus."* That is God's purpose for elevation!

ENOUGH IS ENOUGH!

In a heavily populated region of India that is mostly Hindu and Muslim, I have friends in ministry where Christian pastors

---

[4] http://en.wikipedia.org/wiki/John_Wesley

[5] http://en.wikipedia.org/wiki/Martin_Luther

are routinely beaten and imprisoned. This family's son who was afflicted with polio as a child, had to wear leg braces. Because of their Christian faith, their neighbors hated and continually mocked them to their faces.

One day the woman next door ridiculed the mother by saying, "What kind of God is this you serve? If your Jesus is who He says He is, He would heal your boy."

I don't have to tell you, that Mama got mad! Angrily, she walked into the house, pulled the braces from her son's legs and told God, "Here he is! You either heal him or take him!" (I have to wonder what her son was thinking at that moment!)

That was it! Having her fill of the status quo, she stood up and took authority over that infirmity. At times, an extreme situation must arise for believers to reach the point of declaring to spiritual wickedness, "Enough is enough! I'm not taking this anymore. It stops right here!"

Not only was her son healed, but a spiritual breakthrough began. One of the greatest revivals in that country can be traced to an angry mother's exercise of her authority as a believer!

Some may mistakenly believe that the moment this mother prayed, she persuaded God to heal her son. That is not what happened. She did not have to *convince* God to heal him. He had determined to heal the boy before he was ever born. When Jesus allowed the Roman soldiers to beat His back with whips 2,000 years ago, He purchased the healing for our bodies.

Because the healing was already there, she simply had to rise up, use her authority to grasp it, and refuse to let go!

IT'S TIME TO JIGGLE THE DOORKNOBS

Even though they are native to the Khumbu region, the Sherpa people had never climbed Mount Everest until alpinist expeditions began. Tradition taught that since the upper regions of the mountain were the gods' dwelling places and to disturb the gods who ruled these heights was dangerous, they remained in the safety of the low-lying areas.[6]

Religious tradition has taught Christians much the same: accept the status quo; stay at base camp; do not jiggle any doorknobs; keep your pew warm until Jesus returns.

But God says you were made for more! You were created in His image to inhabit the uppermost regions of the Kingdom. Places have already been prepared. Keys to His 'many rooms' are in the next pages of this book. So, go ahead . . . turn the key!

---

[6] http://adventure.nationalgeographic.com/adventure/everest/everest-quiz/

Chapter 6

KINGDOM KEYS: GAIN AUTHORITY OVER SPIRITUAL DIMENSIONS

E levation occurs when you take authority, first over your own life and then the twelve spiritual dimensions in the following chapters. Taking authority over your life requires confronting the enemy head-on, and then telling him you are on the way to a new level.

I mean it when I say, "Tell him!" Use the power residing in your voice. Just open your mouth and declare that God's plans for your life are about to be manifested. No, the enemy will not like it, but what can he do about it?

> *"Be sober, be vigilant; because your adversary the devil walks about like a roaring lion, seeking whom he may devour"* (1 Peter 5:8 NKJV).

There is a big difference between the three letters in the word 'can' and the word 'may.' *Can* deals with ability, while *may* is about permission. In the verse above, Peter does not merely say you have an enemy; he is warning you to be mindful of him ("be sober; be vigilant").

The enemy will never ask permission to devour your life; nor will God give the enemy permission to hurt one of His children. Permission can only come from *you*. But if you can *grant* permission, that means you can also *deny* it.

Denying the enemy permission into your life could very well be your first exercise of authority. Of course, he will not be happy that you have discovered this authority. He may growl, snarl, and show his teeth, but he cannot touch you without your permission.

The Kingdom keys Jesus promised in Matthew 16:9 for opening spiritual dimensions are known as "breakthroughs." Once you understand that skillfully learning to exercise your authority can help you ascend to higher dimensions, no door will remain closed to you!

Levels of spiritual authority are much like the steps of a staircase in our Father's house, each containing 'many places to stay.' However, you will not move from step one to the top landing. You arrive by placing one foot before the other and methodically moving higher and higher. The next chapters deal with personal revelations and my observations of other believers who have moved upward in these spiritual dimensions.

Since God has already elevated and *"seated you with Him in the heavenly realms in Christ Jesus,"* each dimension will manifest as you take authority in the spiritual realm. The following pages will explain exactly how to do that.

Chapter 7

AUTHORITY OVER SELF
"Up Out of the Mud"

*"He lifted me out of the slimy pit, out of the mud and mire;
He set my feet on a rock and gave me a firm place to stand."*

Psalm 40:2 NIV

Authority over self is the bedrock of your ascent upward—and the first dimension of spiritual authority that you must master. Spiritual footings must be set upon *the* Rock and then deepened and fortified by exercising authority over the flesh, emotions, and thought life. To experience breakthrough in the consecutive spiritual dimensions, you will always need that *"firm place to stand."*

Because of the constant danger of spiritual abuse, God requires you to master authority over self before trusting you with higher dimensions. Those who fail to conquer self are more likely to slip into *coercive* authority, which at its very core is *cultic*. (Yes, I said 'cultic'!)

Spiritual breakthroughs do not occur at this first level; rather, this level *prepares* you for breakthroughs in all other spiritual dimensions.

You can faithfully tithe, attend church, learn to pray, lead a Bible study, or worship in a manner that rocks heaven's throne. But unless you take authority over self, you will remain stuck in the foyer of God's House of many rooms. Even though you entered through *the* door, subsequent doors will not open without the proper key.

MORE THAN THE FLESH

Religion has always equated authority over self as the 'taming of fleshly lusts.' But, that is only a *portion* of self and is not associated with elevation.

The powerful tool of fasting is more than a physical practice. Fasting also involves your thoughts and emotions. If you should disagree, try fasting a favorite food for a few days. You will soon be daydreaming and longing for that crawfish étouffée—even if you're not physically hungry.

Through their strict rituals, the Pharisees subdued many of their fleshly cravings, but they made no progress in the Kingdom. Taking authority over self requires a spirit-controlled life, which was impossible for them.

Much like the good religious leaders of every age, the Pharisees were outwardly doing everything right. But Jesus saw the pitiful condition of their thoughts and emotions:

"Woe to you, scribes and Pharisees, hypocrites! For you are like whitewashed tombs which indeed appear beautiful outwardly, but inside are full of dead men's bones and all uncleanness" (Matthew 23:27 NKJV).

Jesus never minced words. Peeling back the façade of these religious hypocrites, He publicly announced that they were nothing more than filthy tombs filled with decaying bones.

A spirit-controlled life, which religion can *never* achieve, attacks the source of the problem. As Paul wrote,

"Those who belong to Christ Jesus have crucified the flesh with its passions and desires" (Galatians 5:24 NIV).

It's those appetites of the flesh *"with its passions"* (or emotions) that we're dealing with. Emotions are the offspring of thoughts. So, to conquer the flesh, we must first control our thoughts and emotions.

Three things will help you achieve authority in this first spiritual dimension:

1. **CHOOSE YOUR FRIENDS CAREFULLY AND PURPOSEFULLY.**

    The impact of those you allow to influence you cannot be overemphasized. Think what happened when these people chose the *wrong* friends:

    - At the urging of a 'friend,' King David's son, Amnon, raped his own sister. For this disgrace, two years later his brother, Absalom, vengefully murdered Amnon (2 Samuel 13).

- 'Friends' of the prodigal son persuaded him to make decisions that led to his financial, physical, emotional, and spiritual ruin. Had it not been for the love of his father, the prodigal would have died in humiliation, eating rubbish with the swine (Luke 15:11-24).

- By choosing wrong 'friends,' Demas, the protégé and likely successor of Paul, deserted the apostle, and forfeited his destiny (2 Timothy 4:10).

Most of us find it difficult to choose appropriate friends because of our warped thinking:

What we *assume* friends will do:	What true friends do:
• Think just like me.	• Balance and challenge you.
• Never say anything that would hurt my feelings.	• Love enough to tell you the truth, even when it hurts.
• Follow me all the way to the pit and back.	• Prevent you from falling into the pit—by force, if necessary.
• Always have fun together.	• Laugh—and weep—with you.

2. TRAIN YOUR THOUGHTS

In His infinite mercy and love, God found you while you were lost, wretched, and undone. You did not go looking for God; He came searching for you! And guess where He found you?

"He picks up the poor from out of the dirt, rescues the wretched who've been thrown out with the trash" (Psalm 113:7 The Message).

Because God made you in His image, your thoughts—like His—have creative potential.

You may have never pictured God as a 'dumpster diver', rummaging through old newspapers, coffee grounds, and KFC buckets, but that is exactly how He found you. Rolling up His sleeves, He reached way down into that miry muck, pulled you out, washed you in Jesus' blood, wrote your name in the Book of Life, and then seated you in the heavenly realms with Christ!

Here's the problem: After leaving your dumpster dwelling, you want to hang onto your old thought processes. Because God made you in His image, your thoughts—like His—have creative potential. If your thoughts are not based on what He says, they will create a future far different from what He intended.

"For as he thinks in his heart, so is he" (Proverbs 23:7a NKJV).

Because you were born into a fallen world, ruled by a fallen lord with deadly ideologies, your brain must be reprogrammed with invigorating thoughts and beliefs.

Notice what Paul wrote to the church at Ephesus:

"... you must no longer live as the Gentiles do, in the futility of their thinking. They are darkened in their understanding and separated from the life of God because of the ignorance that is in them due to the hardening of their hearts...That, however, is not the way of life you learned when you heard about Christ... You were taught, with regard to your former way of life, to put off your old self, which is being corrupted by its deceitful desires; to be made new in the attitude of your minds; and to put on the new self, created to be like God in true righteousness and holiness" (Ephesians 4:17-24 NIV).

Science has proven that through a neurological process, hormones and chemicals interact to produce tiny electrical currents. Thoughts are created through these neurological pathways in the brain.

Much like the hardwiring in a computer, your brain (computer) has been programmed in a world ruled by death. This means that your neurological pathways, or 'the way you think' was hardwired the wrong way. When you enter the Kingdom, God begins installing a new wiring system.

Studying God's Word creates thoughts that form new neurological pathways. The more you read His Word and think His thoughts, the deeper these pathways become.

While everything is going well, your thoughts easily travel up and down these new pathways. But when you approach a difficult situation and things become tough, your brain reverts to its original wiring.

All the time you have been laying new paths, the old ways remain. Since the new ways are not traveled as often as the old, your brain chooses the path of least resistance.

The good news is, as God's Word gradually replaces the negativity and wrong thinking, new pathways become more deeply etched. Finally, the brain permanently rejects the old paths in favor of the new.

Tradition tries to prohibit your ascent by locking you into 'the way things have always been.' Never allow the excuse, "it's just the way I was raised," to remain. Some of those ways were just plain wrong. After all, if you compared this fallen world to heaven, we *all* came from a dumpster!

In case you thought this journey would be easy, think about this:

> *"We demolish arguments and every pretension that sets itself up against the*

*knowledge of God, and we take captive
every thought to make it obedient to Christ"*
(2 Corinthians 10:5-6 NIV).

The word 'captive' gives a clue that this will take some work on our part. Thoughts are not that compliant or obedient. If they were, Paul would have calmly instructed us to align our thoughts with God's Word. Instead, he chose a combat term that says we must forcefully seize every thought that contradicts God's Word.

Some pathways have deep ruts; some traditions have become deeply entrenched; some thoughts will not leave without a fight. To forge a new path, you must read, think, and speak God's Word—and then do it again and again.

3. **RULE YOUR EMOTIONS.**

Approximately 85 percent of decisions are based on feelings rather than logic. Since decisions will determine the course of your life, those statistics from the field of psychology are frightening.

If so many of life's decisions are based on emotions rather than reason, how confident are you that the route you are traveling will lead to God's intended destination?

We master our emotions by controlling our thoughts. And as discussed, thoughts are controlled by purposely being aligned with God's Word. Having authority over emotions is definitely a sign of spiritual strength.

> *"He who is slow to anger is better than the mighty, and he who rules his spirit than he who takes a city"* (Proverbs 16:32 NKJV).

However, the opposite is also true.

> *"Whoever has no rule over his own spirit is like a city broken down, without walls"* (Proverbs 25:28 NKJV).

Allowing yourself to be controlled by emotions is nothing short of witchcraft, which is defined as: emotional manipulation of thoughts and actions. Feelings have nothing to do with your salvation or your position in Christ. That is why Paul admonished to: *"Walk by faith, not by sight"* (2 Corinthians 5:7 NKJV).

A person can destroy their own life if emotions alone are in control. If your logic and feelings are not in alignment, reject your emotions and proceed down the path of reason.

WORTH A THOUSAND WORDS

The brain is more powerful than the most efficient computer ever constructed by man. But unlike the computer, the brain does not comprehend in abstract terms or a series of numbers. It thinks in pictures. Shut your eyes and think about someone who is important to you. The letters of their name will not be printed on a black background. What you see will be a picture of their face as you last remember them.

Test this theory at your next family reunion. Uncle Boudreaux may have gained fifty pounds and lost all his hair since you last saw him. The reason for hardly recognizing him is that his image was recorded in your memory as a smaller guy with more hair.

Your friends, thoughts, and emotions are powerful determiners of your self-image. The way to change images of yourself is to choose friends who will reflect the truth about you, have thoughts that agree with what God says about you, and who refuse to control your emotions.

Aligning the brain's immense power with what God sees and says will help you achieve the physical, mental, and emotional discipline to exercise authority over self. Practice seeing yourself as God sees you:

- His forgiven child;

- unconditionally loved;

- whole and healed;

- elevated with Christ;

- possessing the ability to exercise authority over spiritual dimensions, both now and into eternity!

Chapter 8

AUTHORITY IN THE FAMILY
"Remember the Lord"

"Therefore I positioned men behind the lower parts of the wall, at the openings; and I set the people according to their families, with their swords, their spears, and their bows."

(Nehemiah 4:13 NKJV)

The second dimension is spiritual authority within the family.

This battle for authority in the family continues to rage. At times, it is between the parents: Dad demands to be 'king of the castle,' while Mom sneers at the mere thought of bowing to such a monarch.

At times, the battle is between parents and children: imperfect parents (as we *all* are) demand submission and respect from rebellious, impudent offspring, intent on overthrowing the current regime.

Regardless of how the battle is exposed, it *always* exists between the enemy and the family. And the outcome is more crucial than you may have imagined. The family is unmistakably indispensable for God's Kingdom purposes to be fulfilled—not just for you and your children, but all humanity. That sounds like a bold statement, so let me explain.

GOD'S DWELLING PLACE

In ancient times, the walls of a city were ultra-important since this was their first line of defense. In fact, they even constructed their homes so that one external wall of a dwelling became a portion of the city wall.

Nehemiah was assigned the task of rebuilding the walls of Jerusalem, which became a blueprint for rebuilding the church. The city had been so demolished, only small piles of rubble remained of her mighty walls. The gates were burned, the Temple was decimated and its treasures ransacked. What few houses remained were nothing more than hovels. Practically nothing was recognizable of her former glory.

The parallel between Jerusalem and the church of today is glaring, yet no cause for despair. You see, God's commitments are irreversible. Jerusalem had remained desolate for years, but God had not forgotten His promise to dwell there.

Likewise, God's commitment to the church is irreversible. As He chose a few faithful workers to rebuild Jerusalem, so He will use a remnant of believers to become the unblemished Bride of Christ. Restoration of the church begins with taking authority in the family.

A FAMILY AFFAIR

To rebuild the wall, Nehemiah assembled the workers by family. Each family had an assigned place to begin. If a family failed to complete their project, the wall would have a breach where the enemy could enter and plunder not just one house, but the entire city.

Because of the integral relationship between individual dwellings and the city wall, one depended upon the other. Likewise, strong churches and strong families are synonymous.

UP TO HIS OLD TRICKS

During the construction, Nehemiah's enemies ridiculed and hatched plots to destroy their progress.

> *"But it so happened, when Sanballat heard that we were rebuilding the wall, that he was furious and very indignant, and mocked the Jews. And he spoke before his brethren and the army of Samaria, and said, 'What are these feeble Jews doing? Will they fortify themselves? Will they offer sacrifices? Will they complete it in a day? Will they revive the stones from the heaps of rubbish—stones that are burned?'...Now it happened, when Sanballat, Tobiah, the Arabs, the Ammonites, and the Ashdodites heard that the walls of Jerusalem were being restored and the gaps were beginning to be closed, that they became very angry, and all of them conspired together to*

come and attack Jerusalem and create confusion" (Nehemiah 4:1-2, 7-8 NKJV).

When Nehemiah learned of the conspiracy, he stationed families along the wall, armed with "swords, spears, and bows" (Nehemiah 4:13 NIV). The laborers literally held a weapon in one hand and a tool in the other (Nehemiah 4:16-18).

The enemy's efforts to destroy you never cease. A favorite battleground has always been the family. Let's face it, he frequently uses the family as a tool for chaos and strife.

Contrary to past teaching on this subject, both men and women serve in a priestly function in the home. Paul taught that in the Kingdom, there is neither male nor female (Galatians 3:28). Gender has no connection with the priestly position.

> **The church defeats the enemy by uniting generations.**

However, this does not diminish the importance of male leadership in the home. It will always be the man's role to lead (Ephesians 5:23). In Nehemiah 4:13, men were placed in forward positions on the wall, yet they were never alone. Working side-by-side and standing guard with the patriarch was the matriarch with their children.

The church defeats the enemy by uniting generations. Because the enemy understands the relationship between family and church, he is determined to worm his way into your family and usurp your position of authority. Do not let him!

GOD'S PLANS FOR STRONG FAMILIES

S trong families are built when unified parents exercise godly authority over their children. Such families are crucial to God's Kingdom purposes for myriad reasons:

1. **To bless generations**

   Our omnipresent God sees the world through a multi-generational lens. When He looks at you, He also sees your ancestors and offspring. When He speaks a blessing, He does not merely address you, but your children and grandchildren. This is why He refers to Himself as "the God of Abraham, Isaac, and Jacob."

   God spoke many promises to and about Abraham: his name would be great, he would be the father of a great nation, his offspring would be as numerous as the stars, and my personal favorite—through him, the whole world would be blessed. That is elevation!

   But Abraham had to meet prerequisites for those blessings to be released. He had to move away from base camp to a land he had never seen (Genesis 12:1), his name had to be changed (Genesis 17:5), then Abraham and every male in his household had to be circumcised (Genesis 17:9).

   By precisely obeying His requests, God knew Abraham could be trusted for the promised elevation:

   > *"For I know him, that he will command his children and his household after him, and they shall keep the way of the Lord, to do justice and judgment; that the Lord may*

bring upon Abraham that which He hath spoken of him" (Genesis 18:19 KJV).

The reason for Abraham's supernatural elevation did not result from taking authority over himself—though he often did so—but because he could be trusted to exercise spiritual authority over his family.

Still, the best news was not about Abraham, but the blessings God would shower upon his children, their children, and ultimately the whole world. When you move from authority over self to authority over family, blessings are unleashed for generations to come!

2. **To teach generations**

The family is God's ideal classroom. This is where children should learn about:

- **God's nature**

  - **Commitment**: by observing parents' commitment to each other and the family, children learn about God's commitment to us.

  - **Discipline and correction**: when parents consistently demonstrate that wise choices produce happiness and poor choices produce pain, children learn about God's discipline and correction—and to make wise choices.

  - **Forgiveness:** by experiencing it from their parents, children learn about God's forgiveness and unconditional love.

- **God's Word**

  - Since God created the home before the church, it was never His intention for the church or a school to be responsible for teaching children His Word.

- **Value**

  - Parents can daily live God's Word before a 'live' audience. And never forget that they watch as closely on Friday night as Sunday morning!

  - The family who values their children begins to understand God's value for them. Again, the natural must come before the spiritual. Children must be taught that they are uniquely created, loved and valued because of their individuality. What a great inoculation against peer pressure!

- **Destiny**

  - Jewish families often introduce their small children as, "This is my daughter, the heart surgeon," or "This is my son, the nuclear physicist." These parents understand the power of speaking destiny over their children! Teach your children that they are created with a one-of-a-kind destiny for which they are responsible to pursue, preserve, and protect.

- **Connect and belong**

  - In the home, children learn about relationships, commitment, and to be discriminate about choosing their friends—and eventually, a spouse. They also learn the value of being surrounded by supportive members, thus the importance of the church.

- **Worship and pray**

  - I learned how to pray by watching and listening to my grandmother. Like most children, I was a reluctant student, but when I grew up and discovered the true significance of prayer, you'd better believe I was grateful for her example. Your children are listening. Make sure when they are 'standing in the need of prayer'—and that day *will* come—they will know what to do.

- **Serve others**

  - Waiting on your children hand and foot does not teach servanthood. It teaches them to be lazy and selfish. Servanthood is taught by participating in chores and daily duties that make the home function smoothly. Parents set the tone through cheerful service to each other.

- **Giving**

  - The home is where children learn the value of obedient, joyful giving. Always let your children know that you tithe, give to missions, and help the needy. When you speak about giving, make it a family affair by using inclusive, plural pronouns, such as 'our' and 'we,' rather than 'I.'

- **Forgiveness**

  - You'll never have to teach a child how to tell a lie. They come fully equipped with a Ph.D. from our fallen ancestor, Adam, and the genetic mutation called 'sin.' When God saves us, we understand His forgiveness by experiencing it. But more importantly, the family teaches us how to give it to others.

3. **To Judge Generations**

This final purpose for the family may sound severe until you understand that its core is all about mercy.

Scripture and experience indisputably reveal that no sin forever remains hidden. A price must be paid for all iniquity. Through His mercy, God has established seven levels of judgment:

- Self-judgment

- Family judgment

- Peer judgment

- Church judgment

- Civil court judgment

- Angel judgment

- The Great White Throne judgment

It is God's desire that all sin be resolved at the lowest level, since the punishment at each stage becomes more severe. Rest assured, all sin will be dealt with at one level or another. As they say, 'the wheels of justice turn slowly, but grind exceedingly fine.'

An Example _Not_ to Follow

Despite his many strong qualities, King David was an atrocious father. The lives (and deaths) of his sons Amnon and Absalom are examples of what *not* to do concerning judgment in the family.

Amnon raped his sister. Apparently, David had surrendered authority in his son's choice of friends, since the act was committed through the encouragement of Amnon's "friend."

Continuing to abandon his parental duties, David failed to make unrepentant Amnon suffer the consequences of his sin. The results were catastrophic.

Because David ignored his family's disgrace, Absalom took matters into his own hands and killed his brother. Again, when confronted by his son's sin, David did nothing. Even the priests (judgment of church) neglected their duty to reprimand Absalom's sin.

The fifth level of judgment was for Absalom to appear in court. Despite his father's pleas for mercy, he should have been tried and executed for his sin. But even if David had successfully begged for his son's life, Absalom still would not have gone free. No one ever does.

You Do Not Want to Go There!

The final two levels of judgment are much more severe. You really do not want to go there!

Angels do not mess around regarding sin:

- Genesis 19: Two angels pronounced final judgment on Sodom and Gomorrah because of their exceeding sinfulness. Both cities were annihilated by fire from heaven.

- Numbers 22: An angel plainly warned Balaam, the disobedient prophet, that if his donkey had not turned aside in the path, Balaam would have already been dead and the donkey spared! Apparently, angels have a low opinion of wicked prophets.

- Daniel 4: According to the decision of "the watchers" (a.k.a. angels), for refusing to repent of his sin, King Nebuchadnezzar roamed the fields and ate grass like an animal.

As horrible as angelic confrontation may be, the Great White Throne judgment is much worse. In every sense of the word, this is the final level.

- Revelation 20:11-12: God is on His Throne, reading from the Book of Life and judging the dead according to what they have done. Two chapters later, we read this chilling, final verdict:

"He who is unjust, let him be unjust still; he who is filthy, let him be filthy still; he who is righteous, let him be righteous still; he who is holy, let him be holy still" (Revelation 22:11 NKJV).

That's it. No more chances to make things right. After every other level of judgment has been ignored, the unjust will forever be unjust.

This is why the family's role in judgment is so crucial. It is the family's responsibility to deal with sin to prevent a higher level of consequences. Should you fail to exercise your authority to judge loved ones, judgment will be escalated up the hierarchy until it has been dealt with, one way or the other!

If you love your children (and grandchildren), force them to take responsibility for their sin. If you do not, it will be someone who does not love them as you do or show the mercy you would.

THREE LITTLE WORDS

Living courageously for your family is not easy, but the results are predictable. If you fight for your family, God *will* protect them.

When the laborers in Jerusalem heard about the enemy's plot to destroy the city wall and their homes, Nehemiah spoke three words: "Remember the Lord" (Nehemiah 4:14).

Never be swayed by pessimism or some wicked 'Sanballat.' Stay focused on God. By making Him your heart's dwelling place, nothing can touch you:

> *"Because you have made the Lord, who is my*
> *refuge, even the Most High, your dwelling place,*
> *no evil shall befall you, nor shall any plague come*
> *near your dwelling"* (Psalm 91:9-10 NKJV).

To live without fear during a raging battle requires preparation and assurance of the outcome. Do not wait for a family crisis to conduct family devotions. Do not wait for the battle to end before giving a victory shout. We shout *for* the victory, not *because* of it!

At the end of the day, it's all about God. He wants to elevate your family, as He did Abraham's, so others will want to join *His* family. The family is imperative to building the church and attracting others to the Kingdom.

Authority in the family is fundamental in the spiritual realm. Once you have learned this lesson well, you have positioned yourself for breakthroughs in higher altitudes of the Kingdom.

Chapter 9

AUTHORITY OVER SECULAR AFFAIRS

"Get back on your horse!"

"When the righteous are in authority, the people rejoice;
But when a wicked man rules, the people groan"

Proverbs 29:2-3 (NKJV)

I f it seems that the world has 'gone to the dogs,' it has to be *our* fault. Now that I have your attention, allow me to clarify.

After creating the world, God handed it to Adam. It was all his. He was the man in charge—until the serpent tricked Adam into giving up the deed to the property.

The church has incorrectly taught that Adam's disobedience resulted in the loss of his relationship with God. What really happened was this: he willingly surrendered not only the right to rule and worship, but the loss of his relationship with God.

Satan is shrewd and his motives cleverly calculated. If he could cunningly tempt man to disobey God, Adam's authority would by default become his, making him the god (little "g") of this world.

For a time, the plan worked. But God had His own strategy of recovering what was lost. His strategy was to send His Son, the 'second' Adam.

As cagey as Satan may be, on his best day he is no match for God. In his prideful thinking, the devil set out to destroy the second Adam, never realizing that Jesus' sacrificial death and resurrection would win back the world for all eternity!

God's plan succeeded. Jesus snatched the deed from the devil's slimy grasp and transferred it to His church. And what have we done with it? Look around for the answer.

THE ENEMY'S SUCCESS, OUR FAILURE

The enemy has somehow convinced the church that an interest in 'worldly' things, such as; science, government, education, finance, the arts, or technology, is an evil motive that leads to our destruction. For too long, we have allowed him to distort God's righteous commands into concepts that promote self more than a lost world.

Please do not consider this as an indictment against the church. Darkness has permeated the foundations of our faith for so long, it is time to expose his evil schemes to the light. My goal is to reveal Satan's diabolical methods so we can regain our God-mandated authority in secular affairs!

THEY NEED US!

The church is not 'excess baggage' in today's world. It is fundamental to the survival of our culture, our nation, and our world. They need us!

It's time to reclaim our rightful position as heirs to all Jesus won from Satan on the cross. We have been duped into believing that a desire for prosperity and influence is evil; that we should silently accept life on the bottom of the heap. That is not scriptural!

> *"If you fully obey the Lord your God and carefully follow all His commands I give you today, the Lord your God will set you high above [elevate] all the nations on earth. The Lord will make you the head, not the tail. If you pay attention to the commands of the Lord your God that I give you this day and carefully follow them, you will always be at the top, never at the bottom"* (Deuteronomy 28:1, 13 NIV; parenthetical mine).

No parent is pleased when a child settles for a life of drudgery through fear or laziness. Parents want their children to use God-given talents and resources to succeed and to elevate their lives.

Our heavenly Father is no different. He desires and *expects* you to use His resources to fulfill your destiny. Remaining at base camp not only fails to attract others to the Father, it also displeases Him!

> *"However, if you do not obey the Lord your God and do not carefully follow all his commands and decrees I am giving you today, all these curses will*

*come on you and overtake you...The foreigners
who reside among you will rise above you higher
and higher, but you will sink lower and lower.
They will lend to you but you will not lend to
them. They will be the head, but you will be the
tail"* (Deuteronomy 28:15, 43-44 NIV).

The fact that the church is ridiculed and slandered around
the world is proof that we have not only miserably failed to rule
His world, but we have actually invited His censure. Clearly, we
have become 'the tail.' Even worse, many are content to stay there.

HOW IS THAT WORKING FOR YOU?

Y ou only have to turn on the television or read the newspaper
to realize that secular leaders' strategies are not working.
To make matters worse, the church has adopted the strategy
of sticking our figurative 'heads in the sand' and ignoring the
world's dizzying downward spiral.

When Pharaoh faced an impending famine that could
destroy Egypt, his advisors were clueless and useless. He needed
someone with a new strategy . . . and that someone was in
Pharaoh's dungeon!

*"The plan seemed good to Pharaoh and to all his
officials. So Pharaoh asked them, 'Can we find
anyone like this man, one in whom is the spirit of
God?' Then Pharaoh said to Joseph, 'Since God
has made all this known to you, there is no one so
discerning and wise as you. You shall be in charge*

of my palace, and all my people are to submit to your orders. Only with respect to the throne will I be greater than you.'

So Pharaoh said to Joseph, 'I hereby put you in charge of the whole land of Egypt.' Then Pharaoh took his signet ring from his finger and put it on Joseph's finger. He dressed him in robes of fine linen and put a gold chain around his neck. He had him ride in a chariot as his second-in-command, and people shouted before him, 'Make way!' Thus he put him in charge of the whole land of Egypt. Then Pharaoh said to Joseph, 'I am Pharaoh, but without your word no one will lift hand or foot in all Egypt' (Genesis 41:37-44 NIV).

Knowing that when the unrighteous rule, chaos and turmoil will abound and suffering will increase, God wants to transfer authority over secular matters to His church, just as Pharaoh did to Joseph.

"There is an evil I have seen under the sun, the sort of error that arises from a ruler: Fools are put in many high positions, while the rich occupy the low ones. I have seen slaves on horseback, while princes go on foot like slaves," (Ecclesiastes 10:5-7 NIV).

God loves His world. He knows that when His children are in charge, the suffering of the weak is diminished (Proverbs 29:2), resources are wisely used to benefit all, there is liberty in worship, and His Kingdom will flourish. That's what it's all about!

L'ENVERS, CHER!

The sound of the Louisiana language where I grew up is almost musical. Still today, some folks predominantly speak this mixture of Spanish, French, and English commonly known as Cajun French.

> To achieve our mission of taking the message of salvation to the world, it's time we get back on our horses!

The French term 'a l'envers' is transmuted in the Cajun vernacular into simply 'l'envers.' It means 'upside-down and backwards.' This is how the Cajun French would describe the verse above where slaves rode on horseback while princes walked like slaves. It is so at odds with how things *should* be, you'd just shake your head and exclaim, "L'envers, cher!"

This topsy-turvy arrangement has never worked for the world or the church, and it certainly has not prospered in the Kingdom. To take authority in secular affairs, you must reject traditional religious teaching that forbids God's people to get involved in politics, health care, entertainment, education, finance, and every other area.

Someone will rule in these areas. And it's impossible to rule while walking like a slave. To achieve our mission of taking the message of salvation to the world, it's time we get back on our horses!

Chapter 10

AUTHORITY WITHIN A MINISTRY STRUCTURE
"But it shines just like gold!"

"Then the blind and the lame came to Him in the temple, and He healed them. But when the chief priests and scribes saw the wonderful things that He did, and the children crying out in the temple and saying, 'Hosanna to the Son of David!' they were indignant"

(Matthew 21:14-15 NKJV).

B rass and gold are difficult to tell apart—at first. They look and feel alike, but the similarities end there. Gold is a precious metal, while brass is an alloy made from copper and zinc. Gold will not tarnish; brass will tarnish and in time, become crystallized, brittle and useless. If you want a metal with an enduring benefit, look for the real deal.

To exercise spiritual authority in a ministry structure, you must distinguish between the authentic and the counterfeit. Genuine spiritual authority in a ministry structure will permanently transform lives, advance the Kingdom, and elevate lives. Counterfeit spiritual authority, which sadly abounds in today's church, is at best, useless; at worst, it can seriously wound others.

The ultimate test to distinguish between gold and brass is to place a drop of nitric or muriatic acid on the metal. Brass will immediately change to a dark color. Gold is completely unaffected. Jesus is the acid test for true spiritual authority. Understanding how He manifests His authority will help you distinguish whether a ministry is brass or gold.

SOME THINGS NEVER CHANGE

Several times a year, Jewish pilgrims were required to travel to the Temple at Jerusalem to sacrifice their best animals. For some, it was a long, tiring trip. By journey's end, their selected animal was often not in pristine condition.

Recognizing this problem, the religious leaders instituted a program to allow merchants to sell flawless sacrificial animals at the Temple. When first conceived, the plan was helpful and practical. But eventually, greediness crept in.

When Jesus arrived in Jerusalem for Passover, His attention immediately focused on merchants selling sacrificial animals for three or four times their value. Those who had come empty-handed had no choice but to pay the ridiculous prices. Enraged by what He saw, Jesus entered the Temple, turned over the merchants' tables, and called them 'thieves' as they fled for their lives (Matthew 21:13 NKJV).

Some religions incorrectly use this story to say that anything sold at a place of worship angers the Lord. However, Jesus did not protest the sale of animals for an important need. What provoked His fury was the greed that had crept into an otherwise beneficial plan.

Immediately after clearing the Temple, two things happened:

> *"Then the blind and the lame came to Him in the temple, and He healed them. But when the chief priests and scribes saw the wonderful things that He did, and the children crying out in the temple and saying, 'Hosanna to the Son of David!' they were indignant"* (Matthew 21:14-15 NKJV).

In recounting the same event, Mark says the religious leaders were more than 'indignant':

> *"And the scribes and chief priests heard it and* ***sought how they might destroy Him; for they feared Him,*** *because all the people were astonished at His teaching"* (Mark 11:18 NKJV).

True spiritual authority:

- is bold, but never coercive.

- gets your attention without intimidation.

- attracts people like flies to honey.

- infuriates and frightens religious people.

Jesus had a habit of attracting the spiritually hungry and scaring away the religious. Nothing about that has changed in the past two thousand years.

THE EXPERT COUNTERFEITER

God is not involved in everything people claim Him to be. For a time, some ministries can flourish without a trace of true spiritual authority. The leaders of these religious organizations are fanatical about *appearing* spiritual. Substituting rules for relationship, they use coercion to control.

> The goal of religion is to control others by creating an appearance of spirituality.

Religion is like counterfeit spiritual authority. It's all about appearance. True spiritual authority is about relationship—and relationship is about connection.

God hates religion. The goal of religion is to control others by creating an appearance of spirituality. That's nothing short of witchcraft, which completely contradicts God's nature by seeking control, not connection.

The basis of God's relationship with you is love. If He were a control freak, He would never have included His irrevocable gift of the free will. He will eternally honor that gift of the ability to choose.

He does not want you to seek or serve Him if it's based on coercion or fear. That is the exact opposite of His Spirit. He will love you all the way to the grave, but never force His will upon you.

He will woo and pursue, but at the end of the day, it's your choice whether or not you follow Him. Joshua summed it up well: *"Choose for yourselves this day whom you will serve"* (Joshua 24:14 NIV).

RELIGIOUS SPIRITS: JEZEBEL AND AHAB

People who manipulate and dominate are attempting to impose *their* will upon others rather than *free* will, which is a direct violation of God's principles. Those who operate in Satan's domain are under the influence of a Jezebel or an Ahab spirit.

On the surface, these ministries look and feel genuine. But once you look past the shiny exterior, they are nothing more than a cut-rate imitation.

Do not allow names to fool you. Since fallen angels are asexual spirits, men and women can be susceptible to either. It just happens that the examples from 1 and 2 Kings are wicked Queen Jezebel and her husband, King Ahab. In our day, two prime examples of a Jezebel spirit are Jim Jones and David Koresh—same spirit, different gender.

The Jezebel spirit uses fear, manipulation, intimidation and coercion to control others. This could involve the 'cold shoulder' or 'silent treatment' rejection, either explicit or implied. As a pretense, they also use the false claim of 'spirituality' for their 'word' from God, prophecy, dream, or vision.

Eventually, this spirit afflicts its followers with depression and self-doubt. Though Elijah was a powerful prophet of God, after his encounter with Jezebel, he became so depressed he wanted to die (1 Kings 19:4).

GOD'S 20/20 VISION

On the other hand, an Ahab spirit is more subtle than the overt, control freak Jezebel, making it even more dangerous. In fact, an Ahab spirit often manipulates a Jezebel, which is what happened in 1 Kings, chapter 21.

The vineyard next door caught the eye of King Ahab. He offered to buy this beautiful piece of property from Naboth, but he was not interested. So what did Ahab do? He went home and began to pout.

> *"So Ahab went home, sullen and angry because Naboth the Jezreelite had said, 'I will not give you the inheritance of my ancestors.'* **He lay on his bed sulking and refused to eat.** *His wife Jezebel came in and asked him, 'Why are you so sullen? Why won't you eat?' He answered her, Because I said to Naboth the Jezreelite, 'Sell me your vineyard; or if you prefer, I will give you another vineyard in its place.' But he said, 'I will not give you my vineyard'"* (1 Kings 21:4-6 NIV).

It's hard to believe that a grown man could act like a three-year-old. But Ahab was no babe in the woods. He knew exactly what he was doing, and got exactly what he wanted.

True to her nature, Jezebel manipulated and schemed until Naboth was brutally executed and then delivered the 'good news' to Ahab (1 Kings 21:8-15). Once Naboth was dead, Ahab suddenly recovered and went to inspect his new vineyard. But no sooner had he left his chariot than Elijah appeared with a sobering message:

> *"This is what the Lord says: 'Have you not murdered a man and seized his property?'"*
> (1 Kings 2:19 NIV).

God saw it all. Knowing the culprit behind the scenes, He charged Ahab with Naboth's murder.

Every Ahab "master manipulator" has a hidden agenda. Their angle is to deceive others into doing their dirty work so they always appear innocent and spiritual. Ever so cautiously, they encourage wrongdoing, but always with sufficient distance from the actual deed to claim ignorance and innocence. I suppose they think God is wearing opaque sunglasses these days.

FIELD GUIDE FOR DETECTING RELIGIOUS SPIRITS

Religious spirits have several distinct characteristics. But before proceeding, let me caution not to judge the guilty too severely. They are probably some of the most wounded people you will ever encounter.

Once their self-worth is so severely injured, they will search for value and acceptance in all of the wrong places. Skillfully controlling others seems the ideal way to gain significance and worth. But it would not prove that this person is the real enemy.

Another word of warning: at some time or other, we can all display these attitudes. Since we are all subject to wounding others or others wounding us, this does not necessarily demonstrate the existence of a Jezebel or Ahab spirit. Be careful not to look too diligently for a particular friend or family member in this list, or you just might find yourself!

Finally, doing your work with excellence does not mean you have a control problem. Nor does avoiding confrontation mean you condone wrongdoing. It's all about degrees and motivation. But, if you meet someone who displays the majority of these traits most of the time, run!

- Takes credit for everything
- Uses other people to accomplish their personal agendas
- Has difficulty apologizing
- Uses information from others to make themselves appear more spiritual
- Is charmingly deceptive
- Doesn't want anyone to disagree with them
- Criticizes others behind their back
- Practices 'one-upmanship'
- Acts superior to others
- Talks incessantly about themselves
- Every situation becomes 'spiritual'

- Is rebellious and refuses to submit to true spiritual authority

- Is 'pushy'

- Operates in 'mysticism'

- Sows seeds of discord and division

- Must be the center of attention

- Attempts to make others 'the problem'

- By withholding approval, causes others to worry whether they're 'measuring up'

- Uses self-pity to get their way

- Treats those who disagree with coldness to force them to submit

- Exaggerates and dramatizes situations

- Uses another's deep emotional hurts to manipulate, while creating strong soul ties with that person

- Puts words in another person's mouth

- Loves titles for themselves and labels for others

- Has a vengeful attitude

WHY IT MATTERS

I don't have to tell you evil is running rampant. You know that just by opening your eyes every day. What I'm saying is that nothing will get better until believers learn to exercise true spiritual authority in ministry structures.

God specifically created the church to confront evil and deal with all its pain and suffering. A dangerous trend we have already examined is that of believers abandoning the local church. Of course, this thrills the enemy because he understands the synergy in God's Word that says: "one can chase a thousand and two put ten thousand to flight" (Deuteronomy 32:30 NKJV).

Researchers have studied group synergy for years. What they have discovered is that teamwork produces "an overall better result than if each person within the group were working toward the same goal individually." [7] What they should have done was to read Deuteronomy 32:30. Since God invented synergy, this verse explains that the synergistic effect of believers working in concert is a multiple of ten.

THE SOLUTION IS IN SYNERGY

In our day, not only has the church been slandered by non-believers, it is often discounted and ignored by professing Christians. Deflating the importance of being part of a local congregation is like saying God did not know what He was talking about when He warned us not to forsake "the assembling of ourselves together. . ." (Hebrews 10:25 NKJV).

The solution to the pain caused by evil is not another church program—and definitely not forsaking the church. The solution is the synergy that occurs when true spiritual authority is present in ministry.

---

[7] http://en.wikipedia.org/wiki/Synergy

How do you produce true spiritual authority within a ministry structure? In case you do not agree with the answer, blame the writer of Hebrews:

> *"Obey those who rule over you, and be submissive, for they watch out for your souls, as those who must give account"* (Hebrews 13:17 NKJV).

Authentic spiritual authority always flows from being *under* authority. If the thought of submitting to spiritual authority in a church angers you, it could be that a spirit of religion from your past has tainted your thinking. As mentioned before, if you recognize one of those religious spirits, run the other way!

BECOME AN AGENT OF CHANGE!

When Jesus drove out the moneychangers, He did not abolish the Temple; He merely cleaned it up. What followed was revival! After Israel had remained in a state of apostasy for hundreds of years, with just one act of true spiritual authority, the blind could see, the lame could walk, and people began to *believe* again!

Believers are the agents of change that our world desperately needs. It's not the omission of God's ordained methods of dealing with pain and suffering, but the cleansing of religious spirits that have perverted God's work—and then submitting to true spiritual authority within that structure.

Never fear submitting to authority. Jesus continually submitted to the Father.

With the present condition of our world, this assignment may appear overwhelming. And you are so right—if we try to do it solo. We must have God's synergy to accomplish all He has asked us to do. We need each other and the world *desperately* needs us!

Chapter 11

AUTHORITY OVER DEMONIC SYSTEMS
"The problem behind the problem"

"For though we live in the world, we do not wage war as the world does. The weapons we fight with are not the weapons of the world. On the contrary, they have divine power to demolish strongholds."

(2 Corinthians 10:3-4 NIV)

The next level, spiritual authority over demonic systems, reminds me of Whac-A-Mole. In this arcade game, plastic moles randomly pop up through holes in a waist high table. The goal is to whack the mole on the head with a soft mallet before it disappears into the hole. But every time you swat the mole in one hole, it pops up in another. It keeps the player busy, but never accomplishing much.

In the church's warfare against demonic systems, our armor is often no more than a 'mallet' of good intentions and righteous indignation. No sooner do we swat at the devil in governmental affairs with an email campaign or petition than he pops up in our educational system. Quickly, we make posters and protest at the next school board meeting, just as his ugly head pops up in the legal system. While we swat away, he keeps ducking. Yes, we are staying busy, but not accomplishing much.

THE WORK OF DEMONIC SYSTEMS

> A demonic system is any organization or deep-rooted methodology that prevents us from having a relationship with God.

The enemy knows that God greatly desires to have a strong relationship with His people. An empowered, authorized child of God spells doom and destruction for the kingdom of darkness. By offering us a substitute, he does everything in his very limited power to prevent that from happening.

A demonic system is any organization or deep-rooted methodology that prevents us from having a relationship with God. Since God alone is omniscient and omnipresent, Satan and his demonic forces cannot be everywhere at the same time. But they have successfully infiltrated the world's systems to distract us from putting God first in our lives. Look around, and you'll see what I mean:

- An education system that teaches our children there is no God to undermine the work of Christian parents seeking to instill morality and godly character;

- An entertainment system that flaunts sinful lifestyles and openly mocks scriptural values;

- A judicial system bent on removing any connection between God and our country's founding principles of godliness;

- A legislative system that sanctions abortion and same-sex marriage;

- Religious systems that are: (1) controlled by a Jezebel or Ahab spirit; (2) so entrenched in tradition, revelation has become nonexistent; (3) promoting false teachings that prevent spiritual maturity;

- A banking system that enslaves the masses and benefits only a privileged few;

- Governmental systems full of greed and corruption that lead to poverty, murder, and genocide.

Demonic systems can become so imbedded in a culture, society is led to believe that it cannot comfortably function without the demonic influence. To avoid disrupting the status quo, they even tolerate suffering of the defenseless.

Taking authority over demonic systems is no game. It requires spiritual maturity and extraordinary discernment.

Jesus demonstrated this type authority when He delivered the demoniac at Gadara.

THE MAN IN THE TOMBS

D emons are disembodied spirits. Before God cast Lucifer and his cohorts out of heaven, they had visible bodies. That changed when they participated in his rebellion. Since then, demons roam about, looking for a place to reside.

Scripture says that a man "who had his dwelling among the tombs" was possessed by a 'legion'[8] of demons. Nevertheless, when he saw Jesus approaching, he ran and fell at His feet (Mark 5:1-9).

When Jesus saw the man approaching, He did not flee in the opposite direction, though I'm sure some of the disciples had to resist the urge to turn and run. The man was clothed with nothing but the remnants of shackles (Luke 8:27), and was filthy and bloody from cutting himself with stones (Mark 5:5). Instead of repulsion, Jesus had compassion on this man who desperately needed a relationship with the Father.

When Jesus commanded the demons to depart, they requested permission to enter a nearby herd of swine. Once inside the pigs, which apparently were intelligent enough to prefer death over demon-possession, they ran headlong down a cliff and drowned in the sea (Mark 5:10-13).

This should have been the happy conclusion to a sad story, but it was not. When the town leaders heard about losing

---

[8] A legion of men was 6,000. While there's no way to know if there were 6,000 demons present in this poor soul, it's safe to say it was more than a few.

their herd of swine, they became so afraid (Mark 5:15; Luke 8:35), they begged Jesus to leave.

Raising swine was the backbone of the economic system of this non-Jewish region. What they apparently feared was a disruption in the status quo that would affect their finances. They were so enslaved to an economic system that valued money over humanity, they preferred that Jesus leave well enough alone. "Let the demoniac continue to suffer; just don't mess with my paycheck." You do not have to look far to see that the Gadarenes are still among us.

The church's mission is not merely to deliver the man in the tombs; the society imprisoned by demonic systems also needs deliverance. Until now, the enemy's strategies have kept us busily swatting the symptoms without ever confronting the system. That is all about to change!

> **You do not have to look far to see that the Gadarenes are still among us.**

THE FIRST RULE OF COMBAT

As Christ's representatives, we alone have the legitimate right to address demonic systems operating behind the scenes. When confronted by demonic powers, we must follow His example: *cast them out!* But if you think the enemy will leave without a fight, think again!

While I would not intentionally draw unnecessary attention to him, one of the first rules of combat is: 'Know your enemy.'

Before addressing these powers, we must first discern who they are, just as Jesus determined what was happening among the Gadarenes.

Our inability to recognize the enemy's face has been part of the struggle—and with good reason. He is a 'shape-shifter'—seen as a serpent in Genesis, an angel of light in 2 Corinthians, and the beast in Revelation.

Shape-shifting is part of his deceitful nature. Jesus said, *"There is no truth in him. When he lies, he speaks his native language, for he is a liar and the father of lies"* (John 8:44 NIV). Our enemy is falsehood personified!

In his bag of tricks is the power to deceive people into believing he does not exist and that those who believe in him are simply superstitious or uneducated. Of course, he would like nothing better than for men to disregard his existence.

SPIRITUAL WHAC-A-MOLE

Major indicators that demonic systems abound are: drug addiction, child pornography, gang activity, abortion, human trafficking, HIV, terrorism, false religions, poverty, alcoholism, same-sex marriage, divorce, suicide, and more. This list of demonic by-products is far from complete.

If Satan can keep us focused on our problems, he knows we'll stay occupied in a 'spiritual' Whac-A-Mole. Jesus' encounter with the demoniac of Gadara taught us to adjust our focus, and then go after the problem *behind* the problem!

Living in one of the most evil regimes in history, Apostle Paul had a two-fold strategy for tackling 'the problem behind the problem': prayer and lifestyle. His prayers moved the Hand that controls the world, and his lifestyle demonstrated that Jesus has something much better to offer!

Paul never led a march, instigated a boycott, or participated in a letter-writing campaign. But he was *definitely* an agent of change. Before we proceed, let me state that I do not oppose marches, boycotts, or writing letters. If you are involved in any protest activity, do not stop. But do not stop there, either!

God has called us to be agents of change—but not merely the favor of a local school board or government official. Real change comes when the herd of swine plunges into the sea and society rejoices over a tremendous deliverance. No petition on earth can be inclusive enough, no protest march large enough, or no letter-writing campaign elaborate enough to achieve that type of change. This change can only occur when believers begin to exercise spiritual authority over 'the problem behind the problem.'

To take full authority over this shape-shifter demonic system, the church must formulate some new strategies. Here's a starting point:

1. **Offer something better**

    When unbelievers examine your lifestyle, is it so attractive they begin to say, "Give me some of that!" Or do they say, "Thanks,...but no thanks!"

    When Peter and John healed the lame man at the Temple, "*He jumped to his feet and began to walk. Then he went with them into the temple courts, walking and jumping, and praising God. When all the people saw him walking and praising God, they recognized him as the same man who used to sit begging at the temple gate called Beautiful, and they were filled with wonder and amazement at what had happened to him"* (Acts 3:8-11 NIV).

The witnesses of this miracle were the very ones who had demanded Jesus' crucifixion. Yet when one man was completely restored, *"many who heard the message believed; so the number of men who believed grew to about five thousand"* (Acts 4:4 NIV).

Just as the lame man jumped for joy in the Temple courts, every elevated life has the ability to inspire 'wonder and amazement' and draw people to Jesus. When they recognize that Jesus offers a better hope, a better joy, and a better life than all those dreadful demonic systems, who would not want to change?

Our assignment is to let them know that Jesus offers more comfort than alcohol, a higher 'high' than drugs, more satisfaction than material possessions, and a deeper relationship than a one-night stand. If they fail to see it in *us*, they will never see it!

2. **Live in obedience to God**

It doesn't take much sense to know that we can't command the devil to leave the entertainment system if we've stashed several adult magazines in a secret place. Obedience begins by mastering the first dimension of spiritual authority: your flesh, thoughts, and emotions.

You can't order the enemy to leave governmental or education systems if he has free rein in your home, secular affairs, or ministry. He will just laugh in your face and go right on about his business. Obedient living gives a legitimate right to look the enemy in the eye and tell him to get out of the way!

Paul knew that an obedient life that honors God produces change. He also knew that if believers live according to the truths Jesus taught, the world would change—not through force, but choice. Obedient living is a double-edged sword: it gives you the right to tell the devil to vacate the premises, while displaying to the world an attractive alternative for its demonic systems.

3. **Pray and fast with purpose**

Just as the natural realm is subject to certain laws, such as Newton's laws of gravity and motion, the spiritual realm also has laws. As a spirit being, Satan is subject to principles that govern the spiritual dimension. One such principle, after you gain authority over self, is that breakthrough in other realms is now possible.

Our enemy is delighted when we associate fasting with ineffective, outdated, legalistic church practices. Of course, this same devil wants you to believe that he doesn't exist. The truth is, fasting and praying *with purpose* spells his doom because you are learning how to take authority over self.

'With purpose' means your intellect has now formulated a *strategic* plan for prayer and fasting. At times, fasting can be 'crisis driven.' While that type of fasting has its own time and purpose, I am referring to a lifestyle of deliberately choosing a certain day (or days) of the week to deny the physical appetite and devote additional time to prayer.

To exercise true authority, you must first be *under* authority. Fasting and prayer *with purpose* brings the entire self—body, thoughts, and emotions—under subjection and opens the way to take authority over all spiritual dimensions, especially the demonic.

The purpose for fasting is not to put pressure on God. Rather, it puts pressure on the flesh by forcing self into submission. This gives you authority to deal with 'the problem behind the problem.'

CLAY JARS AND TRUMPETS

Two thousand years ago, Jesus explained how real change occurs in demonic systems when we address 'the problem behind the problem.' From the world's point of view, victorious spiritual warfare is impossible to achieve. Fortunately, we do not see or do things their way.

Using a clay jar and trumpet as weapons of warfare would seem to be a formula for absolute defeat. But for Gideon's army, it became God's victorious strategy.

For years, the Midianites had methodically oppressed Israel, destroyed their livelihood, and intimidated them to the point of hiding in caves. Then God told Gideon, who was the weakest member of Israel's weakest clan (Judges 6:15), to choose 300 unarmed men to fight against thousands of armed

Midianites. Gideon's warriors could only take a trumpet and a torch concealed in a clay jar.

Obediently, Gideon and his men confronted the Midianites by night. When the signal was given, the men blew their trumpets, broke the clay jars, and let their lights shine. The Midianites were so frightened and confused, they began to destroy each other. It was a stunning victory for Gideon's army!

> *"But we have this treasure in earthen vessels, that*
> *the excellence of the power may be of God and not*
> *of us"* (2 Corinthians 4:7 NKJV).

You are God's clay jar. Within you is the Light of the world. By breaking the jar, or taking authority over self, God's glory can shine through. This is how the lost are attracted to His goodness and we annihilate the enemy's darkness. Come out of your cave! Let the Light of Christ shine!

Chapter 12

AUTHORITY OVER RESOURCES
"God wants to give you something"

"The silver is mine and the gold is mine,
declares the Lord Almighty"'

(Haggai 2:8 NIV).

I van Petrovich Pavlov won the Nobel Peace Prize in 1904 for creating a better understanding of conditioned responses with dogs. His experiments consisted of ringing a bell every day, just before feeding the dogs. After a time, when the bell was rung, it triggered the dogs' digestive processes, whether or not food was present.

Since people share these 'Pavlovian responses,' the mere reading of this chapter title probably evoked one of the following reactions:

1. You got excited, thinking I was about to say that God wants to pour money into your bank account to purchase a bigger house or new car.

2. You unconsciously sneered at the thought of me saying that God wants to pour money into your bank account to purchase a bigger house or new car.

3. You became angry at the thought that I would ask you to give more money to my ministry so that God can pour money into your bank account to purchase a bigger house or new car.

With so much inaccurate teaching pervading the church about God and resources (a.k.a. money), any of these responses is understandable. Most teaching on finances errs toward one of these extremes: *prosperity* teaching says that God wants to shower us unconditionally with money, while *austerity* teaching says that we exalt God by doing without or gracefully suffering for His cause. While both are partially correct, the element of truth in each theology does not mean this is what God intended. There is also a third position.

BEHIND DOOR NO. 3

Scripture is chock-full of God's promises for financial blessings. While these blessings are conditional, the condition is **not** suffering.

> *"Now it shall come to pass, if you diligently obey the voice of the Lord your God, to observe carefully all His commandments which I command you*

> *today, that the Lord your God will set you high above all nations of the earth. And all these blessings shall come upon you and overtake you, because you obey the voice of the Lord your God"* (Deuteronomy 28:1-2 NKJV).

- *"God will set you high above all nations"* speaks of your elevation.

- *"Because you obey the voice of the Lord your God"* refers to the prerequisite for elevation.

I am not advocating legalism or religion. While you can do nothing to *earn* God's blessing, you must exercise obedience to possess spiritual authority.

God wants to bless you. Both Scripture and experience reveals this is true. Even so, nowhere does Scripture imply that the purpose of His blessings is to satisfy personal desires. That is often a gratifying by-product of His blessing, but not the primary purpose.

God knows that any sustained elevation would require taking authority over financial resources. Before your birth, He knew your destiny. At the time of your birth, He released the necessary resources to complete your assignment. Since those resources already exist, you must exercise spiritual authority to release them into your life. In fact, it's the only way your accomplished mission can bring glory to God.

SERIOUS SIMOLEONS

Because God's reputation is at stake, funding your elevation has to be part of His plan:

*"And you shall remember the Lord your God, for
it is He who gives you power to get wealth, **that
He may establish His covenant which
He swore to your fathers,** as it is this day"*
(Deuteronomy 8:18 NKJV).

Performing His Word is crucial. Since He has promised
that His people will be a blessing to the whole world, fulfilling
that promise will require more than rummage sale money.
Supernatural resources are required.

The literal translation of the word "power" means *wealth*.
God has promised to give wealth so we can obtain *more* wealth.
He is fully aware that it takes money to make money. So, the
whole purpose for providing start-up funds is to *"establish His
covenant which He swore to your fathers"* and to make His people a
blessing to the whole world!

EXACTLY WHAT WE NEED

Building the Kingdom will require enormous financing,
whether it's an orphanage in Africa, a church in India, or
an inner-city outreach in America. As Christ's representatives
on earth today, we have the same supernatural authority over
resources as He had. That's a good thing, since that type of
authority is mandatory to fulfill our assignment.

Consider a few ways Jesus exercised supernatural authority
over resources:

- With these simple words, two disciples were
  dispatched to find a colt (donkey) that had never been

ridden: "The Lord needs it" (Mark 11:1-3). If you question whether that command was supernatural, consider that the price of a donkey was equivalent to a new Cadillac Escalade. How many people could say to a stranger, "The Master needs your vehicle," and they would cheerfully give it away?

- On at least two occasions, Jesus fed tens of thousands of hungry people with a few loaves and fishes (Matthew 14, Matthew 15, Mark 6, Luke 9, John 6). If you have teenagers in your family, you have a much clearer understanding of the significance of this miracle!

- By following Jesus' instruction, Peter caught a fish with a coin in its mouth that could pay tribute for both of them (Matthew 17:24-27). To make this happen, a particular fish had to be supernaturally attracted to an object at the bottom of the lake, develop an insatiable appetite for a metal coin, swim to the spot where Peter had just dropped his line, and then find the bait so irresistible—despite his mouthful of metal, that he would swallow the hook. The probability of being struck by lightning ten times would be greater than this. But it became one of the Lord's modes for releasing supernatural resources.

Jesus wasn't the only one who demonstrated supernatural authority over resources. Throughout Scripture, many divine assignments were linked with supernatural resources:

- Nehemiah's assignment to rebuild the walls of Jerusalem compelled pagan kings to reach into their wallets and extend an American Express Black card. That would be equivalent to North Korea's leader funding a hundred orphanages in Africa. The reason for classifying it as supernatural is that in the natural, it would never happen.

• In a land where the queen would be executed for speaking to the king without his permission, Queen Esther requested and gained authority to elevate her Jewish people in all 127 provinces of Persia and Media. Regardless of the country or culture where God's children may reside, He can still bless them. Though Esther was a Jewish queen, her pagan husband, King Ahasuerus, held all the power. For him to relinquish such tremendous authority to Esther and Mordecai, the cousin who had adopted her, was nothing short of supernatural.

• Because of her obedience, a widow and her son were fed supernaturally every day, while the rest of the country suffered extreme famine. When Elijah instructed her to cook him a small cake from the last remnants of her meal and oil, she obeyed (1 Kings 17:10-15). As a result, for three and a half years, they never lacked food.

Before you have a 'Pavlovian' response to this story and think I'm about to ask you to "sow a seed to meet your need (and fill my greed)," notice these two things:

○ The widow's obedience to God—*not Elijah*—released supernatural resources. *"Then the word*

> *of the Lord came to him (Elijah), saying, 'Arise, go to Zarephath, which belongs to Sidon, and dwell there. See, **I have commanded a widow there to provide for you** '"* (1 Kings 17:9 NKJV).

- ○ God's plan was to provide *for the widow and her son* (again, not Elijah). He could have commanded the ravens to continue supplying the prophet with food (1 Kings 17:2-5), but God's desire was to bless the widow. Elijah became the key who unlocked supernatural resources; but the widow's spiritual maturity, demonstrated through her obedience, released a breakthrough in the dimension of authority over resources.

SUPER SUPERNATURAL

In Cajun dialect, the word *very* may be replaced if an adjective is repeated twice. For instance, if a crawfish boil is particularly spicy, it would be 'hot hot' instead of 'very hot.' Some believe that the African cultures that use this speech pattern adopted it from the slaves who worked the Louisiana plantations[9]. If being sustained for three years in the midst of extreme drought and famine was supernatural, Israel's experience in the desert had to be *super* supernatural.

The desert where Israel wandered for forty years receives less than one-tenth of an inch of rain every ten years. Yet two and a half million of God's people exercised supernatural authority over supernatural resources and flourished for four decades in

---

[9]   http://louisianacajunslang.com/language.html

this inhospitable environment! Every day, they ate angels' food and drank from a river that constantly flowed from a levitating rock that followed them on their journey.

IT ALL BELONGS TO GOD!

Israel's assignment was to build a sustainable society in Canaan. God provided resources for this mission from the gold and silver the Egyptians willingly gave as Israel was departing from their land (Exodus 12:35-36).

I used the word 'gave,' but the truth is, the gold and silver were not theirs to give. The Egyptians were just holding it in reserve until God's people were ready to fulfill their assignment. You see, everything belongs to our Father!

"The earth is the Lord's and the fullness thereof"
(Psalm 24:1 KJV).

Since God is the legitimate owner of **everything**, He can do with it as He pleases. Should that include blessing you, nothing can stop Him!

Taking ordinary measures in ordinary circumstances will produce predictable outcomes. God wants you to move *up* from the ordinary to a realm of supernatural authority over supernatural resources. You are definitely moving up when ordinary actions begin to produce very uncommon results:

- Peter cast an ordinary fishing line into an ordinary lake.

- Nehemiah requested time and money from King Artaxerxes in an ordinary way.

- The widow of Zarephath prepared an ordinary meal in an ordinary way.

God has the will and the right to bless you supernaturally.

Since you have a *supernatural* Father, stop expecting ordinary outcomes! Everything He does is by definition *supernatural.* To do otherwise would be *un*natural for Him.

God has the will and the right to bless you supernaturally. Because everything belongs to Him, it's His prerogative and His nature to bless you supernaturally.

PROOF POSITIVE

It is not extraordinary to drink from a small stream or well in the middle of a desert; but it *is* supernatural for a river to gush from a moving, levitating rock! Eating date palms or desert hares in the middle of a desert is not supernatural; but it *is* supernatural for manna from heaven to be furnished every morning.

Leading Israel through the wilderness was God's way of unequivocally proving that they could trust in His supernatural ability to care for them, regardless of the environment or circumstances (Hosea 2:14).

Rather than responding with awe and gratitude, they grumbled and questioned His motives:

> *"They willfully put God to the test by demanding the food they craved. They spoke against God; they said,*

'Can God really spread a table in the wilderness?
True, He struck the rock, and water gushed out,
streams flowed abundantly, but can He also give us
bread? Can He supply meat for his people?' When
the Lord heard them, He was furious; His fire
broke out against Jacob, and His wrath rose against
Israel, for they did not believe in God or trust in His
deliverance" (Psalm 78:18-22 NIV).

So, He sent fire from heaven and destroyed them. (Not really, but only because God isn't like man). His love, mercy, and grace are beyond our comprehension. Even in His very justified anger, He blessed them:

"Yet He gave a command to the skies above and
opened the doors of the heavens; He rained down
manna for the people to eat, He gave them the
grain of heaven. Human beings ate the bread of
angels; He sent them all the food they could eat"
(Psalm 78:23-25 NIV).

GOD'S GOODNESS

Goodness is the true nature of the God you serve. He so enjoys blessing us, He continues to do so even when we deserve His wrath (which is probably more often than we would care to admit). He never gives us 'just enough to get by;' He gives abundantly: *'all the food they could eat.'*

Not only that—and this will really mess with your religious tradition—God loves and enjoys blessing people so much, He'll bless those who practice unrighteousness to lead them to repentance.

Religion teaches that God is responsible for giving you cancer, taking your first-born, or sending you into bankruptcy, just to make you repent. But that's not what His Word says. The goodness of God—not His wrath, leads to repentance.

The goodness of God—not His wrath, leads to repentance.

"Or do you despise the riches of His goodness, forbearance, and longsuffering, not knowing that the goodness of God leads you to repentance?" (Romans 2:4 NKJV).

KINGDOM CULTURE

Religion and culture will hinder elevation because it keeps you from accepting the bold truth of God's Word.

> *"The Lord will command the blessing on you in your storehouses and in all to which you set your hand, and He will bless you in the land which the Lord your God is giving you"* (Deuteronomy 28:8 NKJV).

Reared in a fallen world, we are indoctrinated with *false teaching* (those last two words might trip you up). Religion has likely taught that you must earn God's approval and blessing, while

American culture teaches that nothing is free. Both philosophies are opposed to God's Word. He did not promise to bless you in the land *when you earned it.* Oh, no! . . . in the land God is *giving* you. He wants to *give* you blessings!

Most believers' minds have been so contaminated with religion and tradition, they fail to grasp this amazing truth. In the Kingdom, His abundant grace gives what we could never work long or hard enough to merit. Quit trying to earn God's blessing. It will never happen!

CONSIDER YOUR WAYS

B y now, I hope you have discovered that the 'something' God wants to give is not a bigger house or a new car. He wants to give supernatural authority over supernatural resources so you can accomplish the supernatural—and permanently elevate your life!

Exercising authority over resources will require: obedience, authority over the preceding dimensions, and reprogramming your thinking.

> *"You have sown much, and bring in little; you eat, but do not have enough; you drink, but you are not filled with drink; you clothe yourselves, but no one is warm; and he who earns wages, earns wages to put into a bag with holes. Thus says the Lord of hosts: 'Consider your ways!'"* (Haggai 1:6-7 NKJV).

If you caught a glimpse of yourself in this verse, I have good news: You are the problem! That is good to know because—you can change. Haggai does not ask you to consider something that is beyond your control; he says to "consider *your* ways" . . . or your way of thinking. If you are dropping money into a bag with holes, the problem is not with God. His ways never need changing. But *mine* do . . and *yours* do!

God *wants* to give everything you need to accomplish His supernatural agenda; but until the holes in your moneybag are repaired, He cannot trust you with His supernatural resources.

Here's a good *hole-mending* checklist:

1. **Believe** that God wants to bless you.

2. **Ask** for the right reasons.

3. **Work** hard in your vocation.

4. **Understand** your assignment.

5. **Use** what He has given you wisely.

6. **Do** everything with integrity.

7. **Honor** God with what belongs to Him.

Chapter 13

AUTHORITY OVER SEASONS
"Crumbs from the table"

"Blessed be the name of God forever and ever, for wisdom and might are His. And He changes the times and the seasons"

(Daniel 2:20-21a NKJV).

South Louisiana has two seasons: the rainy season and not-so-rainy season. The average annual rainfall is a little over five feet,[10] which makes for a lush, green landscape with lots of mosquitoes. Growing up, I couldn't imagine a spot on earth as dry as the desert where Israel roamed for forty years.

Of course, as I grew older and traveled past the borders of my state, I realized how incorrect my perception was. One problem of being part of a fallen race in a fallen world ruled by a fallen lord is that our perception becomes reality. We take for

---

[10] http://www.weather.com/weather/wxclimatology/monthly/graph/70596

granted that what we've seen and heard all our lives is truth—when in fact, it may not be.

Becoming a disciple means emptying your mind of false data programmed into your 'computer' and replacing it with the new reality of God's Word. This is what Paul referred to as "the renewing of your mind" (Romans 12:2).

DON'T RUSH TO JUDGMENT

We have discussed at length the importance of applying truth in our lives. The truth you are about to learn, if applied, will change your destiny. Parts of it may be hard to accept at first, but before you close this book, allow me to build my case.

We have been taught and observed that spring follows winter and autumn follows summer (or the not-so-rainy season follows the rainy season). Without a doubt, we know that's the way it has always been and will always be for everyone. But that is not true.

> *"To everything there is a season, a time for every purpose under heaven"* (Ecclesiastes 3:1 NKJV).

At the first reading, this verse seems to contradict what I just said; but what makes this verse revelatory are the words 'under heaven.' Ecclesiastes, chapter 3, confirms the existence of seasons, but only 'under heaven.' Seasons are a fact of *natural* life. 'Under heaven' is where natural life occurs, where you walk and talk every day—but *not* where you are *'seated.'* Because it is not connected with the element of time, heaven has no seasons.

Here, under heaven, there is a time to sow seeds, a time for seeds to grow, and a time to harvest the ripened seeds. But, that is not the way it has always been, or always will be.

A REASON FOR THE SEASONS

After the fall, introducing seasons into our world was an act of God's grace. In His original design, seasons were unnecessary because of the thick cloud covering surrounding the earth, much like that of the planet Venus. This created a greenhouse effect with a constant moderate temperature and perpetual irrigation. Conditions such as these created a continuous harvest season.

After the fall, everything changed. God cursed the man and the ground he must work to eke out his survival (Genesis 3:17b-19). It was not until after the Flood when Noah offered an acceptable sacrifice that God implemented a season of harvest.

> *"Then Noah built an altar to the Lord, and took of every clean animal and of every clean bird, and offered burnt offerings on the altar. And the Lord smelled a soothing aroma. Then the Lord said in His heart, 'I will never again curse the ground for man's sake, although the imagination of man's heart is evil from his youth; nor will I again destroy every living thing as I have done. While the earth remains, seedtime and harvest, cold and heat, winter and summer, and day and night shall not cease'"* (Genesis 8:21-22 NKJV).

The harvest season is God's reminder to us that even in His justifiable anger He is merciful. It's an annual glimpse backward of how things used to be and forward to how things will be again.

> **The harvest season is an annual glimpse backward of how things used to be and forward to how things will be again.**

From the days of Noah to now, God's irrefutable Word and His seasons stand, giving us the false perception that it's always been that way and always will be. Wrong again:

"'Behold, the days are coming'," says the Lord, 'when the plowman shall overtake the reaper, and the treader of grapes him who sows seed'" (Amos 9:13a NKJV).

Ordinarily there are several months between sowing seed and harvest. Amos tells us that the element of time now restricting the harvest will be removed. Not only will harvest be perpetual, as it was before the fall, but accelerated. Time will no longer govern harvest. According to Revelation 22:2 (NKJV), each tree will yield its fruit each month.

This isn't a lesson in agriculture; but until you understand the natural, you cannot grasp the spiritual.

GOD CHANGES SEASONS

The seasons of life can be times of abundance or scarcity; times of health or illness; times of joy or sorrow. When their lives are elevated, God's people will experience abrupt changes in seasons, both in the natural and the spiritual.

1. ABRAHAM: a maker of idols to founding a nation through whom the whole world would be blessed.

2. ISAAC: planted crops during a famine and reaped a hundredfold harvest (Genesis 26:12), which is rare, even in today's world.

3. ISRAEL: in a hostile, barren land, the nation thrived for forty years.

4. JOB: regained twice what had been lost (Job 42:12-16), which required an accelerated harvest and renewed fruitfulness to father ten more children.

5. DAVID: a refugee, hiding in caves, became the king of Israel.

6. ELIJAH: with a spoken word, broke a three-year drought, which released a season of survival for Israel (1 Kings 18:41-45).

7. ESTHER: was responsible for elevating the status of Jewish people living in captivity, which also prepared the way for a return to their homeland.

8. DANIEL: transformed Israel's 70 years of captivity into freedom.

Elevate Your Life

An accumulation of experiences has convinced the human race that seasons are unalterable. Waiting 'for my time to come' seems to be the only possible choice. That is not so! The God we serve can step in and change our season—regardless of what 'time' it is. He can transform a desert into a lush garden while others frantically search for a small stream to sustain them.

> The God we serve can step in and change our season—regardless of what 'time' it is.

AS A MAN

Jesus regularly changed the seasons of those He met: the demoniac at Gadara, the woman with an issue of blood, the blind and lame in the Temple, the Roman centurion . . . and the list goes on and on.

While holding a few loaves and a couple of fish, suddenly spring, summer, and harvest accelerated in His hands. Sunday School teachers say that Jesus performed this miracle in the role of God. He did not. Though He was fully God and fully Man, Christ had to lay aside His divinity to reconcile us to the Father:

> *"Let this mind be in you which was also in Christ Jesus, who being in the form of God did not consider it robbery to be equal with God, but made Himself of no reputation, taking the form of a bondservant and coming in the likeness of men"* (Philippians 2:5-7 NKJV).

While living on this earth, everything Jesus did was as a Man, completely yielded to His Father's authority. As members of Christ's body, we have the same authority over seasons as Jesus demonstrated. Here is the guarantee:

> *"Most assuredly, I say to you, he who believes in Me, the works that I do he will do also; and greater works than these he will do, because I go to My Father"* (John 14:12 NKJV).

The only prerequisite is submission to the Father's authority.

THE REST OF THE STORY

At the Temple, Peter and John changed the lame man's season by speaking to him a declarative word of faith. And the result? Many believed in Christ; but that was only part of the story! A few verses later, Peter explained that his restoration of health was only the 'knee of the cypress tree'[11] of what Jesus had come to do.

> *"But those things which God foretold by the mouth of all His prophets, that the Christ would suffer, He has thus fulfilled. Repent therefore and be converted, that your sins may be blotted out, so that times of refreshing may come from the presence of the Lord, and that He may send Jesus Christ, who was preached to you before,*

---

[11] A cypress knee is a small portion of the root of a cypress tree that protrudes up through the soil of marshy areas where cypress trees abound. http://en.wikipedia.org/wiki/Cypress_knee

> *whom heaven must receive until the **times of restoration of all things,** which God has spoken by the mouth of all His holy prophets since the world began"* (Acts 3:18-21 NKJV).

True to form, Peter's testimony about Jesus was bold and to the point. More often than not, his approach had caused him trouble. But on this occasion, he clearly declared the importance of repentance—plus another mysterious revelation: through Christ, God had established a season for the *restoration of **all** things.*

The word 'restoration' means: to return something to its original state. Through Christ, man and all creation will return to their original state. That would also include a restoration of the church's authority over spiritual dimensions as demonstrated by Peter and John in the healing of the lame man!

Jesus' death, burial, and resurrection purchased more than a 'Get Out of Hell Free' card. He actually returned us to the original, God-created status before Adam and Eve yielded to the serpent's deception—complete with His delegated authority over *all* lesser realms.

HUNGRY LOCUSTS

Jesus came to restore all that the enemy had stolen and to reverse the consequences of Adam's sin upon creation.

> *"So I will restore to you the years that the swarming locust has eaten, the crawling locust, the consuming locust, and the chewing locust, my great army which I sent among you"* (Joel 2:25 NKJV).

This Hebrew word for 'restore' literally means: "I'm making a covenant with you to *complete what is missing.*" In other words, God is saying, "Whatever is missing because Adam messed up, I'm making a covenant with you to fix it." That covenant was made through the person of Jesus Christ.

THE SECOND ADAM

Jesus came as the 'second Adam' to recover everything the first Adam had lost and to restore all creation to its original state. In the beginning, harvest occurred year-around, which was the reason Jesus expected figs when it was not the right time or season.

While on earth, Jesus' restorative work was set in motion. Being 'a *man* under authority,' He had the legitimate right to exercise authority over all dimensions.

> Elevation requires taking authority over whatever season you are in and then accelerating it.

Because of His authority over seasons, when He approached the fig tree and held out His hand, the fig tree was obliged to align with His authority and produce fruit. When it failed to do so, Jesus cursed the fig tree and it died.

For elevation to occur, each of us must align with and submit to spiritual authority. Otherwise, we will invite the curses the enemy seeks to inflict upon our lives. Elevation requires taking authority over whatever season you are in—or that you're waiting for, and then accelerating it.

121

To exercise spiritual authority over a season means: no more suffering through times of hardship while 'waiting for my ship to come in.' Instead, just step out of your current season into the motor-mounted pirogue that's racing so fast toward the dock, you'll have to leap out of the way to keep God's blessings from 'coming upon you and overtaking you' (Deuteronomy 28:2).

CHANGE YOUR SEASON

M any Christians are convinced that the world has a lot to learn from us—and it does. But the truth is, the world can also teach us a thing or two!

Mark records the story of a Syro-Phoenician woman who so firmly believed in Jesus' power to heal her demon-possessed daughter, her season was accelerated ten years into the future!

Not until Peter preached to Cornelius and his household was the Holy Spirit released to the Gentiles (Acts 10:44-46). This mother's encounter with Jesus was at least ten years prior to the opening of the door for Gentile converts.

> *"For a woman whose young daughter had an unclean spirit heard about Him, and she came and fell at His feet. The woman was a Greek, a Syro-Phoenician by birth, and she kept asking Him to cast the demon out of her daughter. But Jesus said to her, 'Let the children be filled first, for it is not good to take the children's bread and throw it to the little dogs.' And she answered and said to Him, 'Yes, Lord, yet even the little dogs*

under the table eat from the children's crumbs.'
Then He said to her, 'For this saying go your
way; the demon has gone out of your daughter.'
And when she had come to her house, she found
the demon gone out, and her daughter lying on the
bed" (Mark 7:26-30 NKJV).

To set the stage, understand that this woman was of Syro-Phoenician (Syrian and Phoenician, a.k.a. Philistine, a.k.a. Palestinian) descent and blood enemies of Israel—both then and now. Second, her daughter was demon-possessed, probably the result of her nation's religious practices, which included demon worship.

Knowing all this, she asked Jesus for a miracle that would not have been available to Gentiles for another ten years. That took either a lot of nerve . . . or a lot of faith. Considering the outcome, I'd say it was faith.

We like to imagine Jesus walking on water, calming storms, and never offending anyone. I feel sure the manner in which He referred to her people, particularly her daughter as 'little dogs,' was very offensive. What drew Jesus' attention was her refusal to place culture above her need, or to be insulted even when ridiculed.

Taking it all in stride, she halted Jesus' refusal with her meek, persistent reply: *"Yes, Lord, yet even the little dogs under the table eat from the children's crumbs."*

Jesus was so amazed by the faith and humility of this sworn enemy of Israel, He reached ten years into the future and changed her season. If the God we serve will change the season for His enemies, how much more would He do for His children?

Take a lesson from this woman. She would not allow culture, religion, or the bait of Jesus' refusal to harden her heart or stand in her way. Faith and humility will provide a breakthrough in your season, just as they did for her!

Stop waiting for your "time to come" and start believing what the Bible says about Jesus and your relationship to Him. He can take you places you could never hope to attain—including seasons!

Because we have been seated with Christ in the heavenly realm, far beyond time, we have been given authority over the seasons of life. This is reality. This is how Jesus lived as a Man under authority when He walked among us. To elevate your life, this is what He now calls you to do.

Chapter 14

AUTHORITY OVER COMMUNITIES AND REGIONS
"Let it shine!"

*"Again He asked, 'What shall I compare the kingdom of God to?
It is like yeast that a woman took and mixed into about sixty
pounds of flour until it worked all through the dough'"*

(Luke 13:20-21 NIV).

I have been told I'm actually a likeable guy—until I get in the pulpit on Sunday mornings. I really don't intend to make people mad, but before the truth can set you free, it often has to get under your skin. The truth about taking spiritual authority over communities and regions contains elements of that genre.

God has never been interested in saving just a few and letting the rest of the world slip into darkness. He desires to bless and change your season for more than individual happiness.

Everything He does benefits the whole world—believers and unbelievers alike. You are likely reading this book because you have a relationship with Christ; but there was a time when you were also among the unsaved. You entered the society of believers because someone, somewhere, took authority over their community.

Taking authority over communities differs from regions. But since the two are intrinsically interwoven, they have been grouped together for this study.

Communities are fundamental units of society beyond the family. While location is a requirement for membership in some communities (such as a neighborhood, vocation, church, congregation, etc.), many of the communities of which we are a member are not dependent upon geography, such as: gender, ethnicity, political affiliation, etc. Regions, however, are always defined geographically.

Our inclusion in these various communities was not by accident. God placed us there. His plan for reaching the world with the gospel has always involved you and me. Not only is that His plan, He cannot accomplish it without us.

That statement may have raised a few eyebrows. In religious circles, the words "God can't" are blasphemy. Without blaspheming or in any way detracting from His omnipotence, our active participation is an integral part of His plan and purpose.

Without a doubt, if He had wanted to use a different method, He could have. Before the foundations of the world, He factored in the cost of His Son's sacrifice and calculated our role into the equation. God Himself ordained this particular method to save the world, and Jesus left the responsibility of implementing the plan squarely in our hands:

> *"Then Jesus came to them and said, 'All authority in heaven and on earth has been given to me. Therefore go and make disciples of all nations, baptizing them in the name of the Father and of the Son and of the Holy Spirit, and teaching them to obey everything I have commanded you. And surely I am with you always, to the very end of the age'"* (Matthew 28:18-20 NIV).

This direct order from the Most High makes Sunday morning 'pew warmers' a little uncomfortable. They would like to think that saving the world is God's responsibility, and their duty is to wait for Jesus to rapture them away to the sweet bye-and-bye.

For those who take Jesus' command seriously, I have two words before you whip out your passport and book a flight to Mauritania: 'communities' and 'regions.' While we're anxious to change the world, God's plan is to change *people*, who will change their community, their region, their nation, and ultimately, His world.

Just before He ascended, Jesus introduced His strategy:

> *"But you will receive power when the Holy Spirit comes on you; and you will be my witnesses in Jerusalem, and in all Judea and Samaria, and to the ends of the earth"* (Acts 1:8 NIV).

He instructed the disciples to witness first in their community, among those with whom they interacted on a regular basis. From there, the gospel would spread through various geographic regions, and finally "to the ends of the earth."

Just as Jesus had said, the process began a short time later. On the Day of Pentecost, about 120 believers had gathered in one place:

> *"And suddenly there came a sound from heaven, as of a rushing mighty wind, and it filled the whole house where they were sitting. Then there appeared to them divided tongues, as of fire, and one sat upon each of them. And they were all filled with the Holy Spirit and began to speak with other tongues, as the Spirit gave them utterance"*
> (Acts 2:2-4 NKJV).

Before filling the believers, the Holy Spirit "filled the whole house." The very atmosphere where these early Christians had gathered reached 100 percent saturation, until each of them was overflowing!

But it did not stop there. It overflowed the walls of the room (the *community* of believers) and into the streets of Jerusalem. When the people heard—and then saw what was happening, about 3,000 were baptized in the Spirit that same day. And that's how a community can be changed!

THE STORY OF YOUR SALVATION

Like a domino effect, a changed community will affect other communities until an entire region has been touched. In Acts 13, after Paul and Barnabas had preached to the Jews about Jesus, the Word was then released to the Gentile community:

"Then Paul and Barnabas grew bold and said, 'It was necessary that the word of God should be spoken to you first; but since you reject it, and judge yourselves unworthy of everlasting life, behold, we turn to the Gentiles. For so the Lord has commanded us: 'I have set you as a light to the Gentiles that you should be for salvation to the ends of the earth.' Now when the Gentiles heard this, they were glad and glorified the word of the Lord. And as many as had been appointed to eternal life believed. And the word of the Lord was being spread throughout all the region" (Acts 13:46-49 NKJV).

And so began the story of salvation. To fulfill God's Word, Paul and Barnabas first took the message of Christ to the Jewish community, and then to the Gentiles. From there, it "spread throughout the region." Those of us who are not of Jewish descent owe an incalculable debt of gratitude to these two disciples!

Once the gospel had spread throughout the region, it continued to leap across continents into what is now Europe. Then it spread to some of the most hostile, remote parts of the world. But it all began with a group of believers in Jerusalem who took authority over their community.

Before you judge God as 'politically incorrect' (not that He would care) for singling out Abraham and the Jewish race as His 'chosen' people, remember their 'choosing' became the delivery system for blessing the whole world. This worldwide blessing from the people of Israel came through the Man, Jesus Christ.

God, the great balancer of His own books, is absolutely fair. Because He loves the whole world (John 3:16), He will knock on every heart's door so that no one is left out. He merely chose Israel as the people through whom He would fulfill His plan of salvation and restore all things.

> God, the great balancer of His own books, is absolutely fair.

FROM DEMONIAC TO EVANGELIST

How amazing is God's mercy and grace! When the people of Gadara sent Him away, Jesus could have easily written them off. Instead, He lovingly gave them a powerful evangelist:

"The man from whom the demons had gone out begged to go with him, but Jesus sent him away, saying, 'Return home and tell how much God has done for you.' So the man went away and told all over town how much Jesus had done for him" (Luke 8:38-39 NIV).

The miraculous deliverance of the demoniac revealed the malicious economic system of that region. But the Gadarenes felt no need of repentance until they heard the testimony of one of their own.

When Jesus returned later, He was welcomed by exuberant crowds (Luke 8:40, 42b). Apparently, the delivered demoniac did as Jesus instructed. His powerful testimony brought revival to the community and entire region.

God's plan for salvation does not start in some foreign land. It always begins in the 'community' mission field. The delivered demoniac assumed his role was to *go* with Jesus and change the world. However, *staying* in his community revolutionized the destiny of an entire region.

KNOW WHAT YOU'RE UP AGAINST

The delivered demoniac faced serious opposition. The region he was told to evangelize was ruled by an economic system that was so demonically entrenched, even Jesus' miracle-working power did not immediately dislodge it.

A region is a physical area ruled by spiritual forces. To take spiritual authority over a region requires an understanding of the current regime. In his letter to the Ephesians, Paul explained the hierarchal order of the government of darkness and the physical component of each level:

> *"For we do not wrestle against flesh and blood, but against principalities, against powers, against the rulers of the darkness of this age, against spiritual hosts of wickedness in the heavenly places"* (Ephesians 6:12 NKJV).

Through his personal skirmishes with the enemy, apostle Paul gained this valuable intelligence:

1. 'Principalities' are local rulers of communities.

2. 'Powers' are regional potentates.

3. 'Rulers' are lords over domains.

4. 'Hosts' (plural) of wickedness rule over domain leaders.

5. The 'commander in chief' is the enemy himself.

THE BATTLE FOR REGIONS

The enemy's first level of command deals with communities. When enforced at this level, spiritual authority will demand hand-to-hand combat with principalities.

Don't worry. When armed with resurrection power and having experienced breakthrough in previous levels, your testimony can scare demonic foot soldiers to death!

> When enforced at this level, spiritual authority will demand hand-to-hand combat with principalities.

Once you've broken through the ranks of principalities, expect to face powers that have corrupted entire regions of our world. Here are some of the horrifying effects of these principalities:

1. Disease: in the sub-Saharan region of Africa, one in twenty lives with HIV.

2. Famine: in many regions of Asia, Africa, and South America, 15 million people die every year from starvation.

3. Genocide: in regions of the Middle East, ethnic groups are systematically murdered.

4. War: too many battles to list are raging in regions of the world; the total of lost lives—in the millions—may never be known.

This list could go for many pages, but you get the point. If you were thinking that spiritual authority over regions was unimportant, I trust you have now changed your mind.

FABULOUS FUNGUS

In describing your role in the Kingdom, Jesus used the word 'yeast.'

> *"Again He asked, 'What shall I compare the kingdom of God to? It is like yeast that a woman took and mixed into about sixty pounds of flour until it worked all through the dough'"* (Luke 13:20-21 NIV).

Yeast is a tiny, single-celled fungus. Don't be offended by this comparison, but … fungus or not, yeast is powerful stuff.

Yeast acts as a catalyst to change the makeup of flour through its respiration (like you, it breathes oxygen and exhales carbon dioxide) and rapid replication.[12] Recipes differ, but an average three to four teaspoons of yeast (about an ounce), are potent enough to affect five pounds of flour.

The nature of yeast can change its environment—not by being smarter (it's a fungus) or bigger (a yeast cell is about

---

[12] http://www.breadworldcanada.com/sciencehistory/science.asp

one-tenth of a millimeter), but *just by being there*. God has ordained that your very presence will change the environment.

STAY AND CHANGE THE WORLD

Y our life and testimony can change the world, right where you are. God placed you in a certain community because He wants you to be an agent of change… right there.

> *"You are the salt of the earth. But if the salt loses its saltiness, how can it be made salty again? It is no longer good for anything, except to be thrown out and trampled underfoot. You are the light of the world. A town built on a hill cannot be hidden. Neither do people light a lamp and put it under a bowl. Instead they put it on its stand, and it gives light to everyone in the house.* **In the same way, let your light shine before others, that they may see your good deeds and glorify your Father in heaven** *"* (Matthew 5:13-16 NIV).

America is in deep trouble, simply because Christians obsessed with 'saving the world' (whatever that means) have neglected to step out of their front door and shine their light into the shut-in's home across the street, or become salt at the local boys and girls club, or a homeless shelter.

Salt that has lost its flavor will readily accept the status quo in a community. For too long, God's people have cowered in church corners, afraid to raise their voice against the world's amoral systems—with the expected horrific results.

If you aren't pushing for a Kingdom breakthrough in your community, Satan will take over; his troops are trained and ready. Once a community falls, the region will soon follow.

> **Salt that has lost its flavor will readily accept the status quo in a community.**

Take time to discern and assess the communities of which you are a member and then pray for them to turn to God. Don't be afraid to be a gatekeeper. Keep watch to prevent the enemy from infiltrating your domain. Others in the community may not have that authority, but you do!

Don't be afraid to let your voice be heard. Speak up for Jesus with dignity! We certainly have more intellect than yeast, so let's do it!

IT'S ABOUT OTHERS

God sees His beloved world stumbling in utter darkness, with human suffering unchecked in every quarter. You have the power, the authority, and the obligation to lead others out of despair by letting your light shine.

By daily living the victorious life, your 'good deeds' will become the light that leads your community to the Father. Others may never see the goodness of God until they see it in you. Once they do, they will give Him glory . . . and He will rejoice because another child has come home!

Chapter 15

AUTHORITY OVER HEALING

"Fight the good fight"

*"Is anyone among you sick? Let them call the elders
of the church to pray over them and anoint them
with oil in the name of the Lord. And the prayer
offered in faith will make the sick person well"*

(James 5:14-15a NIV).

Ascending new heights will guarantee the challenge of
unfamiliar obstacles. While trekking through these
pages, you've probably felt the discomfort of adjusting to
perilous levels of elevation. If you're struggling against hurricane
force winds, fighting to secure every step, take heart! You are
moving in the right direction!

If you have not yet grasped the thought, you could
contend with some severe opposition at this level.

The enemy knows that nothing so clearly demonstrates God's existence, power, and compassion as the healing of an incurable disease. Because he is so evil, the enemy enjoys watching God's children endure affliction and miserable pain. With all his might, he will fight against healing.

Exercising authority over healing begins with knowing it is real and available—then how to fight for it.

BEQUEATHED TO YOU

A few years ago I traveled, as I do several times a year, to preach in India for long-time friends. The flight to Visakhapatnam in the state of Andhra Pradesh was grueling. Arriving mentally and physically exhausted, my only thought was to find a bed and sleep well into the next day.

The friend who met me at the airport made me wonder what I'd ever done to deserve such a cruel statement: "You have thirty minutes to get ready. We've got a preaching engagement tonight that's a four-hour drive from here."

I would love to say that I had this serene smile and thanked God for such a wonderful opportunity—but I did not! I went straight to my room feeling anything but an inspiration to preach, grumbling under my breath the whole time.

The road where we departed soon ended, but on we traveled making our own road. Finally, we arrived at a farming village where the gospel had never been preached.

As a pastor, I should have been overwhelmed with compassion for the seven to eight thousand who had gathered to hear the good news of Jesus Christ. But to be quite honest, at that moment I didn't care if all India was lost. Dog-tired, I was running on autopilot as I preached one of the shortest sermons of my career.

But while delivering this abbreviated salvation message, I began to hear cries and shouts scattered across the field of the open-air meeting. When I gave the altar call, every person came forward for prayer, which resulted in a supernatural outpouring of the Holy Spirit.

Even though God had mightily moved, my attitude had not improved much. All I could think of was that long, four-hour trip over a non-existent road before collapsing in a bed. That is, until my friend began asking for testimonials. As they began to share, my spirit was humbled beyond words:

- A white-haired farmer, completely stooped from the waist by an injury twelve years ago was now standing erect and praising God!

- A blind man's eyesight had been restored, though no one had prayed or laid hands on him.

- A woman who had been deaf all her life was yelling in the unmistakable nasal tone of one who had never heard a voice: "I can hear! I can hear!"

- A person possessed by demonic spirits had been instantly delivered.

These and many other bona-fide miraculous healings and deliverances were the source of the shouting while I preached. Of course, I could certainly take no credit for anything.

Unquestionably, God had manifested His miracle working power to heal without the aid of me or any other human being.

The same power that delivered the demoniac and healed the blind, deaf, and lame in India is the identical power Jesus exercised 2,000 years ago and bequeathed to **you**: *"...he who believes in Me, the works that I do he will do also; and greater works than these..."* (John 14:12 NKJV).

CONSEQUENCES ENDED!

Healing is for real. It is a provision of the atonement, just as much as our salvation. Jesus' death and resurrection not only saved us from sin, it also delivered us from the consequences of sin.

"The reason the Son of God was made manifest (visible) was to undo (destroy, loosen, and dissolve) the works the devil [has done]" (1 John 3:8 Amplified Bible).

Sickness and disease, the components of 'death,' entered the world when Adam and Eve sinned; healing and deliverance entered when the Second Adam came to restore all things to their original state.

"Surely He has borne our griefs and carried our sorrows;

> **Jesus' death and resurrection not only saved us from sin, it also delivered us from the consequences of sin.**

> *yet we esteemed Him stricken, smitten by God,*
> *and afflicted. But He was wounded for our*
> *transgressions, He was bruised for our iniquities;*
> *the chastisement for our peace was upon Him,*
> *and by His stripes we are healed"* (Isaiah
> 53:4-5 NKJV).

Some say these verses in Isaiah refer solely to the healing of our relationship with God. But every serious Hebrew scholar who reads *"by His stripes we are healed,"* will agree that these words imply *physical* healing.

EXPERIENTIAL THEOLOGY

Those who base their theology on experiences rather than the Word of God are heading for trouble! But the worst part is choosing to live beneath the altitude God intended.

There are several reasons believers struggle with faith for healing:

1. **Healing is no longer available.** Many belief systems today teach that miraculous healings validated Christ's ministry as the Messiah. In the first century, evangelism required a strategy with strong evidence, but the supernatural is no longer necessary for our day.

   The problem with this theory is simple math. When Jesus was alive, there were approximately 250 million people on earth. Today, there are more than 7 billion and half have never heard the gospel. If healings were necessary to reach 250 million, they would be even more critical for the unevangelized 3.5 billion in our world.

However, healing is not just an instrument of evangelism. The purpose of Jesus' miraculous healings was not to prove His identity. Because He was a Man under authority, healings were the result of the physical world aligning with His spiritual power and authority over that dimension.

2. **Supernatural healings are no longer required.** The United States has close to 700,000[13] physicians and surgeons. With so many trained medical personnel, it's no wonder the sick do not ask God for healing. Other cultures and nations who have nowhere else to turn, experience far more miraculous healings.

   If we fail to trust God with small ailments (the flu, viruses, infections), when a major illness strikes, we have no faith to trust Him for healing. I am not suggesting that you discontinue visiting a doctor when you're sick, but why not ask God for healing as well?

   Certain illnesses are beyond the aid of the most knowledgeable, skilled physicians. Should the day come when the family doctor has nothing to offer, you will need the care of an already established Doctor-patient relationship, the Great Physician.

3. **We have the power, but not the authority.** When we stopped believing in or requesting healing, we stopped

---

[13] http://www.bls.gov/ooh/healthcare/physicians-and-surgeons.htm

exercising authority in that dimension. Like the old saying, "use it or lose it," we failed to use it—and lost it!

TAKE IT BACK!

D o not despair! The spiritual authority for physical healing is still available!

- Taking the authority for healing begins with asking. Once our fallen-world hardwiring learned to bypass the option of asking God for healing, our first response when illness strikes has been running to the doctor. It's okay to call the doctor, but reprogram your response by *first* going to God in prayer before calling your doctor.

  "You do not have because you do not ask God" (James 4:2b NIV).

- If healing does not come right away, continue asking. Even Jesus prayed twice for a man's eyesight to be restored (Mark 8:22-25).

  Everything about our walk with God is a journey. Miracles such as those in India were instantaneous. But healing can also be a recovery process.

  *"They will lay hands on the sick, and they will **recover**"* (Mark 16:18b NKJV).

- Learn how to fight wisely in this battle for authority over healing. While our enemy fights dirty, we retaliate with faith.

*"Dear friends, I've dropped everything to write you about this life of salvation that we have in common. I have to write insisting— begging!—that you **fight with everything you have in you for this faith entrusted to us as a gift to guard and cherish"** (Jude 1:3 The Message).*

You have had a 'good fight' when you refuse to quit. The word "fight" in this verse is also translated *struggle* and *contend.* When the odds seem to be stacked against you and there is nothing more the doctors can do, it's time to fall to your knees and contend for authority to heal.

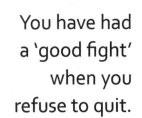

You have had a 'good fight' when you refuse to quit.

UNTIL YOUR LIFE IS POURED OUT

At this very moment, U.S. military personnel are in touch with missile silos that have the power to destroy a substantial part of life on our planet. They wait only for a person of higher rank to give authority to turn a key.

This person of authority is not a private fresh out of boot camp. He is an elderly general with more than a couple of stars on his lapel. Because of his experience and maturity, he has gained the authority.

Having access to spiritual weaponry can annihilate cancer, heart disease, diabetes and HIV. Your Commander wants you to be skillful with these weapons because He understands the devastation caused by sickness and disease. This level of authority requires the maturity to:

- Draw close to God and contend for the breakthrough: *"Keep on asking and it will be given you; keep on seeking and you will find; keep on knocking [reverently] and [the door] will be opened to you"* (Matthew 7:7 Amplified).

- Keep praying and praising even when the test results are unchanged and you're attacked with a barrage of fear and doubt: *"I will bless the Lord at all times; His praise shall continually be in my mouth"* (Psalm 34:1-2 NKJV).

- Believe and confess what your eyes cannot see: *"And they overcame him by the blood of the Lamb and by the word of their testimony, and they did not love their lives to the death"* (Revelation 12:11 NIV).

- Like Christ, serve God and His people until your life is poured out: *"Therefore I will give him a portion among the great, and he will divide the spoils with the strong, because he poured out his life unto death"* (Isaiah 53:12a NIV).

Chapter 16

AUTHORITY OVER DIMENSIONS
"The blood, the anointing, and the glory"

"There remains, then, a Sabbath-rest for the people of God"

(Hebrews 4:9 NIV).

G od's business is to elevate people. He's been doing it since He first chose Abram, a nobody working in his father's idol shop in Ur of the Chaldeans.

The first words spoken to Abraham were about elevation:

"Get out of your country, from your family and from your father's house, to a land that I will show you. I will make you a great nation; I will bless you and make your name great; and you

> *shall be a blessing. I will bless those who bless*
> *you, and I will curse him who curses you; and in*
> *you all the families of the earth shall be blessed"*
> (Genesis 12:2-3 NKJV).

Being elevated from a childless idol-maker to a father of many nations meant that Abraham was destined to break through numerous spiritual dimensions. He was also given the distinct privilege of becoming 'friend' to the God of the universe (James 2:23) and one of the wealthiest, most influential men of his generation.

Now, let's fast-forward 400 years. Rather than enjoying an elevated dynasty in the land of Canaan, Abraham's descendants had been demoted to one of the lowest ranks imaginable—a race of slaves in the nation of Egypt.

Still, God had never forgotten His promise to Abraham. It was no surprise that his descendants were enslaved and mistreated. In fact, God had already foretold both the servitude and deliverance of the Israelites:

> *"Then the Lord said to him, 'Know for certain*
> *that for four hundred years your descendants*
> *will be strangers in a country not their own*
> *and that they will be enslaved and mistreated*
> *there. But I will punish the nation they serve*
> *as slaves, and afterward they will come out*
> *with great possessions. You, however, will go*
> *to your ancestors in peace and be buried at*
> *a good old age. In the fourth generation your*
> *descendants will come back here, for the sin of the*

Amorites has not yet reached its full measure'"
(Genesis 15:13-16 NIV).

HIDING AMONG SHEEP

G od has always been much more
interested in us than we are
in Him. When He spoke to Moses
from the burning bush (Exodus
3:4), Moses had shown no interest in
finding God. In fact, for the last 40
years, he had been hiding in Midian
as an anonymous shepherd.

God has always been much more interested in us than we are in Him.

As usual, God came seeking
for Moses, just as He did for you and
me while our address was still on
Dumpster Lane. His sole purpose was elevation, not just for
Moses, but the entire nation.

> *"Now therefore, behold, the cry of the children of
> Israel has come to Me, and I have also seen the
> oppression with which the Egyptians oppress them.
> Come now, therefore, and I will send you to Pharaoh
> that you may bring My people, the children of Israel,
> out of Egypt"* (Exodus 3:9-19 NKJV).

God's intention was to elevate Israel with a permanent
promotion, just as He wants to keep elevating you from one
dimension to the next. Learning to take authority over each
dimension will assure a continual elevation.

THE LIES OF PHARAOH

Every dimension has its own 'pharaoh' whose assignment is to prevent you from taking authority over your present dimension. Pharaoh's voice will say things like:

- Don't even think about a better job in this tough economy.

- Your marriage is doomed; all you can hope for is a life of misery or divorce.

- Resign yourself to being sick the rest of your life; God will never heal you.

These and other lies are his tools for imprisoning you with a slave mentality. If you break through to a new dimension but fail to take authority, you have merely traded one pharaoh for another.

Taking authority in each dimension is crucial. Without it, you will remain in some form of bondage and never achieve your ultimate elevation.

PHARAOH MEETS HIS MATCH

The children of Israel were Pharaoh's slaves. His job was to forever keep them subservient to his kingdom. In fact, the entire Egyptian economic system depended upon God's chosen people furnishing them with slave labor. L'envers, cher!

Even today, the systems of this fallen world depend upon the enslavement of God's rightful heirs. If the enemy can force His children to dutifully wear their shackles, hang their heads, and make bricks to build the world's systems, nothing will change.

The Egyptian Pharaoh met his match when every Israelite applied the blood of a sacrificial lamb to the doorpost of their home. And that's how *your* pharaoh will be defeated!

The blood of Jesus has become Pharaoh's kryptonite. He will never come near it, because that's what renders him powerless and ineffective.

At every elevation, a greater measure—never less—of the Savior's blood will be required. Each time you break through to a new level of spiritual authority, pray for a fresh covering of the Lamb's blood . . . then watch your Pharaoh run for cover!

WELCOME TO THE WILDERNESS

After Pharaoh's army has drowned in the Red Sea and all the victorious shouting and dancing has subsided, . . . look around. You will have no idea where you are or where you're going. *Welcome to the wilderness!*

In this uncharted territory, you'll quickly discover how desperately you need God. The wilderness will redefine who you are and what your relationship with God really is.

Every level of the journey requires fresh revelation. The image you picture yourself to be must change from that of a stooped-back slave cowering beneath the taskmaster's whip to an heir of God, seated with Christ in heavenly realms.

That's right . . . you must 'see' yourself. When you look in the mirror, what kind of person is staring back at you? Use that supercomputer God placed between your temples to view yourself in the way He intended. Then allow your mouth to speak these words:

> *"I am a forgiven child of the Most High God who has been elevated in Christ. I am healed and healthy. I have a good marriage. My children love and serve God. I have creative abilities and abundant resources to fulfill my destiny. I have authority over my seasons. God has given me authority over demonic spirits and specifically placed me in this community to be His agent of change."*

MORE THAN A DELIVERER

For the Israelites to survive in the Promised Land, they must look to God as more than a Deliverer. Those many years in the wilderness taught them how to *trust* God.

Your cry may be deliverance from a 'pharaoh' of oppression, drug addiction, restoration of a marriage—or even for salvation. But God wants to become more than your Deliverer; He wants to be your 'Lord' and Master.

Navigating through the wilderness requires a stronger, more powerful anointing. Each time a prophet or priest anointed David, a higher dimension of authority was involved. His first anointing was as a youth, then as a leader of men hiding in caves. His third anointing was to govern a single tribe; and finally, to rule an empire. At each new level, he was given a fresh understanding of himself and of God.

Anointing is a by-product of faith, and faith is a by-product of God's Word. The first requirement for dimensional authority always involves immersing yourself in God's Word.

> **The first requirement for dimensional authority always involves immersing yourself in God's Word.**

ACROSS THE JORDAN

B efore sending Moses to deliver the Israelites from Egypt, God introduced Himself at the burning bush.

> *"Moreover He said, 'I am the God of your father—the God of Abraham, the God of Isaac, and the God of Jacob.' And Moses hid his face, for he was afraid to look upon God"*
> (Exodus 3:6 NKJV).

This was no ordinary introduction. God was reminding Moses that His covenant promise with Abraham remained steadfast. The time had finally come for Israel to be elevated.

> *"I have also established My covenant with them, to give them the land of Canaan, the land of their pilgrimage, in which they were strangers. And I have also heard the groaning of the children of Israel whom the Egyptians keep in bondage, and I have remembered My covenant"*
> (Exodus 6:4-5 NKJV).

As revolutionary as Abraham's breakthroughs were, God was about to promote Israel to a level the patriarch had never achieved. Having always been a perpetual tenant, Abraham had never owned property in Canaan. Now, God was *giving* his descendants the land as their inheritance.

Elevation is God's ultimate will for your life, but it's never meant for a single generation. Every breakthrough should be transferred from a parent to their children, and their children, and on and on. Elevation can turn things around for you *and* your heritage.

As preparation for crossing the Jordan River, Israel had to trust God in the wilderness. But to become residents in the Promised Land, something more was required; they had to experience God's glory.

Canaan was not an empty, vacant land awaiting the arrival of new settlers. It was home to half a dozen nations: *"the Canaanites and the Hittites and the Amorites and the Perizzites and the Hivites and the Jebusites"* (Exodus 3:17b NKJV). In their new homeland, Israel had to defeat thirty-one kings (Joshua 12:1-24).

Never were the Israelites the largest, strongest, or most intelligent people. They were simply a nation under Jehovah's authority, completely dependent upon His glory.

In every dimension, God's glory will be responsible for opening doors and crumbling walls. His glory shines brightest when we offer Him our praise and worship. To become a resident in your new elevation, the wisest thing you can do is learn to bask in His glory!

WHAT REMAINS

After defeating thirty-one Canaanite kings, Joshua's next assignment was to divide the land among the people. Each tribe, except the priestly tribe of Levi, received a portion of the Promised Land.

> *"Only to the tribe of Levi he had given no inheritance; the sacrifices of the Lord God of Israel made by fire are their inheritance, as He said to them"* (Joshua 13:14 NKJV).

God's plan was to give the priests a special inheritance: a personal relationship with the God of Glory. Though King David was not from Levi's tribe, his customary worship encounters provided him instant access to treasures far greater than money or possessions.

> *"Oh, Lord, You are the portion of my inheritance and my cup; You maintain my lot. The lines have fallen to me in pleasant places; yes, I have a good inheritance"* (Psalm 16:5-6 NKJV).

A personal relationship with God became David's most treasured inheritance.

As splendid as owning a slice of the Promised Land may be, God wanted His people to explore a dimension far superior to fertile soil. He wanted to be their treasure of inestimable value and for them to cherish a personal relationship with the Lord God Jehovah.

Israel, as a nation, never achieved their ultimate elevation; yet the promise is still available. In this highest dimension of

'Sabbath-rest' (Hebrews 4:9), we can be seated with Christ in heavenly realms. After all, a person who is 'seated' occupies a truly restful position.

MOVIN' ON UP!

E very arena of life has its own successive steps of elevation:

- Academics: GED ... to ... Ph.D

- Athletics: Little League ... to ... Olympics

- Finances: Bank teller ... to ... Warren Buffett

- Technology: Wright brothers ... to ... NASA's space program

- Medicine: Jonas Salk ... to ... modern geneticists

- Entertainment: community theater ... to ... Academy Awards

As you insert the key that takes you from one Kingdom dimension to the next (Matthew 16:19), you will discover "many rooms" (John 14:2). Some of these 'places to stay' may appear to be your Promised Land . . . at least for a while.

Because of God's commitment to elevate, the time will come when you will look around and then say, "You know, this isn't as interesting as it used to be. It's beginning to look a little monotonous."

To feel discontented with the status quo is God's way of beckoning you to the next level. Knowing that more is coming keeps the heart racing and the thrill of expectancy. In the

Kingdom, you never have to remain where you are. Each level holds undiscovered treasures and the joy of fulfillment.

As your life is elevated, so will be the Kingdom. Like the artist who receives praise for creating a masterpiece, your Father is glorified when you excel:

> *"For we are His workmanship, created in Christ Jesus for good works, which God prepared beforehand that we should walk in them"* (Ephesians 2:10 NKJV).

IT TAKES MORE

Traversing the "Balcony of Everest" requires much more skill and commitment than stepping outside your tent at EBC. Since higher elevations involve increased danger of altitude sickness and avalanche, climbers must be more cautious and committed to make it to the next altitude.

Merely presuming that you exist at a higher level than you really do could ensure a short-lived promotion. You will soon be sliding down the mountain toward base camp.

Taking authority over dimensions requires Jesus' blood, His anointing and glory. Each new level always demands more than the last. To experience more of His precious blood requires a greater surrender; more anointing demands a deeper commitment to God's Word; and more glory demands a more intimate worship.

Are you ready for ***more?***

Chapter 17

AUTHORITY WITH GOD OVER NATURE
"Say the Word"

"Marvelous things He did in the sight of their
fathers, in the land of Egypt, in the field of Zoan.
He divided the sea and caused them to pass through;
and He made the waters stand up like a heap"

(Psalm 78:12-13 NKJV).

With a spoken word, God created the worlds. This truth has become fundamental to your faith, but understanding the science behind the statement will revolutionize the manner in which you apply truth. Yes, . . . I did say, 'science.'

From science, we learn that sounds are vibrations. The vibration of a clanging cymbal is different from the vibration of your voice; but both create sounds by displacing air as it passes through.

The speed of the vibration is the *frequency* of the sound. Lower frequencies are associated with slower vibrations, which the brain translates into a deeper pitched sound, and vice versa.

The science of cymatics is the study of *visible* sound and vibration.[14] Looking beyond the invisible effects of air vibrations, it focuses on the tangible effects sound has upon matter. Cymatics "demonstrates the vibratory nature of matter and the *transformational* nature of sound."[15]

Scientists have devised resonance experiments[16] where sound waves of various frequencies spontaneously transform a freely moving medium (i.e., salt, sand, water, rice) into geometric patterns. Notice the higher the frequency, the more complex the shape. As long as the frequency is unchanged, the pattern remains immovable.

These patterns "mirror the symmetries found throughout the natural world, from the hidden shapes buried within snowflakes to the massive hexagonal cloud formations found on Saturn."[17]

HUM A FEW BARS

All these experiments are impressive, but what I found to be most remarkable was a man humming very loudly as he

---

[14] http://en.wikipedia.org/wiki/Cymatics

[15] http://www.cymaticsource.com/

[16] "Amazing Resonance Experiment" http://youtu.be/wvJAgrUBF4w.

[17] http://www.cymatics.org/

leaned over a drum covered in sand. At the sound of his voice, the sand began to line up in geometric patterns, controlled only by the frequency and tone produced by his mouth and vocal chords.[18] The sand patterns and shapes would move in response to even the slightest change in his volume and tone.

While witnessing the power of the man's voice to transform shapeless matter into intricate geometric patterns, I began to see how God created the worlds. As He leaned over and spoke into nothingness, the vibration of His voice caused matter to arise and form the many geometric patterns that make up our universe.

Using more familiar terms, *"Then God said, 'Let there be light'; and there was light"* (Genesis 1:3 NKJV), or to paraphrase in cymatic terms: "Then the vibrations of the Lord's voice caused matter to align into light."

In 1942, Nikola Tesla, a great scientist and engineer of the early 20th century, said, "If you want to find the secrets of the universe, think in terms of energy, frequency, and vibration." I wonder if he grasped how close he was to understanding how God created the universe!

. . . AND HOLDS IT IN PLACE

E very time the frequency of God's voice changed, something unique took shape. And each unique shape remained because God's Word endures.

---

18 http://search.yahoo.com/search?fr=mcsaoffblock&type= A001US0&p=resonance experiment man's voice and drum

*"Your word, Lord, is eternal; it stands firm in
the heavens. Your faithfulness continues through
all generations; you established the earth, and it
endures"* (Psalm 119:89-90 NIV).

The resonance experiments I observed (and would
encourage you to watch) demonstrate how sound waves can shape
matter into patterns, and then hold the matter in a consistent
shape as long as the sound remains unchanged.

As long as God's spoken Word remains unchanged in the
cosmos, so does the result of His Word:

*"He is the sole expression of the glory of God
[the Light-being, the out-raying or radiance of
the divine], and He is the perfect imprint and
very image of [God's] nature,* **upholding
and maintaining and guiding and
propelling the universe by His mighty
word of power"** (Hebrews 3:1 Amplified).

In the physical realm, we call these unchanging life patterns
the "laws of nature." Typically, we find comfort in the fact that
these laws remain constant. However, if you are tumbling down
the side of a mountain, Newton's law of gravitation is anything *but*
comforting. The same is true with other laws of nature:

- Mendel's law of genetics can predict whether your
child will be born with a congenital heart defect.

- Newton's first law of motion says the speeding car
headed your way will not stop until it crashes into
your car.

In situations like these, it is comforting to know that with one word, God can suspend the so-called "unyielding" laws of nature—and that on many occasions, He has given His people the authority to do likewise.

To exercise this God-given authority over nature, you must first understand who you are in Christ, how to submit to spiritual authority, develop spiritual maturity, and become a faithful steward.

TO BUILD YOUR FAITH

Nature has been defined as: the material or physical world surrounding mankind which exists independently of human activities, including all living things. To have authority over nature would include the physical world and all its fundamental qualities.

Throughout the Bible, God exercised His own authority over nature. I'm wondering if His commands could have sounded like this: "Now, hold it right there! I know that I created you to function in a certain way, but in this particular instance, I'm speaking a different command for you to obey."

Notice what happened on these occasions when nature responded to God's command:

- The Red Sea parted (Exodus 14:21).

- Water gushed forth from a desert rock (Exodus 17:6), then that same rock followed Israel through the wilderness (1 Corinthians 10:4).

- The sun stood still and the moon stayed until Israel won a battle (Joshua 10:13).

- No rain fell for more than three years (1 Kings 17:1).

- For three years, meal and oil were multiplied to feed three people (1 Kings 17:16).

- Fire from the sky consumed a sacrificial offering soaked with water (1 Kings 18:38).

- An iron ax head swam to the top of the Jordan River (2 Kings 6:6).

- A widow's jar of oil miraculously filled a multitude of containers. The sale of the oil paid her debt and spared her two sons from becoming slaves (2 Kings 4:1-7).

- When Peter saw Jesus walking on water, he was invited to do the same (Matthew 14:25-29).

- At Jesus' command, a violent storm was calmed (Matthew 8:23-27).

- Jesus raised three people from the dead (Luke 7:13-14; Mark 9:25; John 11:43-44).

- Both Peter and Paul raised people from the dead (Acts 9:36-42; Acts 20:9-12).

- Jesus fed thousands with a few morsels of food (Matthew 14:13-21; Mark 8:1-9)

- After baptizing an Ethiopian eunuch, Philip was miraculously transported to another city (Acts 8:39-40).

Three other manifestations of God's authority over nature could be included that I heard about or personally witnessed:

- Three nurses confirmed the death of a woman. As they spoke with a funeral home director to come for her body, she was suddenly restored to life—in response to the fervent prayers of a group of believers. Before that time, she was the only saved person in her family; afterward, many of them came to Christ.

- In answer to prayer, the missing parts of a man's inner ear suddenly formed. This would be more accurately classified as a creative miracle than a healing.

- During the war in El Salvador, rebels began to disrupt a church service by firing weapons at the worshippers. Miraculously, the bullets passed straight through their bodies, leaving holes in their clothing and the walls—but no one was injured!

- I am acquainted with a military pilot whose helicopter crashed from enemy fire. They killed every person on board and looted their bodies—except the pilot. As he silently prayed, soldiers walked all across the area where he laid, yet ignored him as though he was invisible!

These miracles were included to build your faith. While we are fully convinced of God's authority over nature, remember that you—His child—share this same authority!

THE SHAPE OF THINGS

By His spoken Word, God created every part of the universe and to this day, they remain in place (Psalm 33:6). Likewise, when He speaks a word that differs from our concept of the word 'normal,' His authority alters the predictable outcome of events. I suppose you could say that when He speaks, the 'shape' of things begins to change!

Because you share DNA with the Creator, your words are also creative. Now, you may not create another universe, but you *can* create the world in which you live. While under God's authority, not only can you speak your world into existence, but on occasion, alter the shape of nature.

It may never be necessary for you to halt a tornado or walk on water, but the time may come when you'll need this authority to reverse a genetic disorder for yourself or someone you love, or to stop an out-of-control car speeding your way. Or, it could be as simple as a refrigerator operating far beyond the warranty period until you have the money to purchase a new one.

LARGER THAN LIFE

The immensity of the God you serve is beyond the comprehension of the human brain. He spoke **everything** into existence: every subatomic particle, DNA strand, tiny grain of sand, one-of-a-kind snowflake, blade of grass, tree, mountain, ocean, animal, human being, planet, or galaxy that has ever or will ever exist. Every unique word from the mouth of God individually created and sustained each one.

> *"For my thoughts are not your thoughts, neither are your ways my ways,' declares the Lord. 'As the heavens are higher than the earth, so are my ways higher than your ways and my thoughts than your thoughts. As the rain and the snow*

come down from heaven and do not return to it
without watering the earth and making it bud
and flourish so that it yields seed for the sower and
bread for the eater, ***so is my word that goes***
out from my mouth: It will not return
to me empty, but will accomplish what I
desire and achieve the purpose for which
I sent it"' (Isaiah 55:8-11 NIV).

He watches so diligently over creation, He knows when a sparrow falls to the ground and the number of hairs on your head (Luke 12:6-7). Because His Voice formed all things before you were born (Psalm 139:13-14), He is intimately associated with all your physical, mental, and emotional characteristics.

It takes only one word from such an immense God to alter the laws of nature and transform the shape of your destiny. When He speaks, He changes the unchangeable.

Chapter 18

AUTHORITY TO ALIGN YOUR WORLD WITH GOD'S PLANS
"Hum to your drum"

"Words kill, words give life; they're either poison or fruit – you choose,"

(Proverbs 18:21, The Message).

We live in an age that can measure global communication in a split second. You can turn on the television and watch a volcano erupt on the other side of the planet. Pick up your telephone and within seconds, you're speaking to a sibling on another continent. Hit 'send' on your computer and a new grandchild's photo will suddenly appear in another time zone.

Even more impressive than this split-second worldwide communication is the ability to communicate instantaneously across dimensions.

God inhabits eternity (Isaiah 57:15) in a spiritual dimension outside time and space. He cannot be seen or touched, yet the second you open your mouth to speak, He hears.

> *"This is the confidence we have in approaching*
> *God: that if we ask anything according to his will,*
> *he hears us,"* (1 John 5:14 NIV).

Interaction between the physical and spiritual dimensions is through vocal sound. Because He is God, He could have chosen any method He wished for the spiritual to interact with the physical. But because of us, He chose to facilitate this inter-dimensional relationship with spoken words.

Scripture says we have been created in God's image, then describes Him as a Spirit without a physical body of flesh and bones. The primary characteristic we share with Him is the ability to speak.

God designed words to be powerful and sound to be creative. That is why He formed us in His image with the ability to speak and the authority to create with our words.

HUMAN WORDS

When Jesus met the Roman centurion (Matthew 8:5-13), He 'marveled' at this man's faith to associate authority with spoken words. Being familiar with a dictatorship, he quickly discerned what Israel's religious leaders had not seen: the words of a person who has submitted to authority can become creative, with a life-transforming power.

To redeem humanity, Jesus had to set aside His deity when He came to earth. His deeds and commands had to be those of 'a man under authority.' Consequently, each time air passed from His lungs through His vocal chords and the tongue and lips formed a word, that word had the authority to calm a tempest, heal the sick, and raise the dead.

Like the creative word that Jesus sent to the centurion's home, you can speak words into your world that will create the shape and pattern of your destiny.

WHO IS LISTENING?

Just as the spiritual world responds to the human voice, experiments in cymatics have demonstrated the effects of sound upon the physical world. But never forget, if your spoken words evoke a response from the Creator, you can be sure He's not the only one listening!

Our enemy is so evil, his heart's desire is to ruin us. He will do everything in his power to "steal, kill, and destroy" God's plans to elevate your life. But the good news is, God has not only given us authority over these twelve spiritual dimensions, we also have authority to defeat the enemy. Again, that authority lies in the human voice.

When Jesus' seventy-two commissioned workers returned with their report (Luke 10:1-6), they were elated at the mission's success:

> *"The seventy-two returned with joy and said,*
> *'Lord, even the demons submit to us in your*
> *name,'"* (Luke 10:17b NIV).

Armed with two things—the powerful name of Jesus and the human voice—these rookie evangelists cast out demons and healed the sick. Having never attended seminary or memorized certain scriptures or specific prayers for the demon-possessed, they simply did what they had repeatedly seen Jesus do. When confronted by a demon, they looked it squarely in the eye, opened their mouths and said, "I command you to leave!"

It worked every time! And why shouldn't it work for you?

SAY SOMETHING!

Believers sometimes conclude that because Jesus bound the strong man 2,000 years ago (Matthew 12:29), they can take a wait-and-see approach about their destinies and how He intends to manifest the Kingdom here on earth.

It's true that Christ's crucifixion and resurrection soundly defeated our enemy, but he still contends for the control of our lives. When we fail to exercise our authority of commanding him to leave, we have just empowered the devil.

If you are ignorant about your authority, that also empowers him. While his empowerment is a lie—just as everything else he does, the results are the same. You will learn to tolerate life at an altitude God never intended for you.

> *"Submit yourselves, then, to God. Resist the devil,*
> *and he will flee from you"* (James 4:7 NIV).

This two-part plan in the Book of James makes us victorious: submit to God's authority and resist the enemy. He will stubbornly refuse to leave until you rise up and demand that he goes!

In Acts 16, a demon-possessed fortuneteller followed Paul and Silas as they ministered in Macedonia. Eventually, her words became very annoying:

> *"And this she did for many days. But Paul, greatly annoyed, turned and said to the spirit, 'I command you in the name of Jesus Christ to come out of her.' At that moment the spirit left her"* (Acts 16:18 NIV).

Even though the demon was daily harassing Paul and Silas, nothing happened until Paul *said* something. Once you have the enemy's attention, it's time to tell him a thing or two:

- I am seated with Christ in heavenly realms!

- I am the head, not the tail!

- I am blessed coming in and blessed going out!

- I have a future filled with hope and prosperity!

- I have power and authority over you!

- Get out of my life!

WATCH YOUR MOUTH

Since spoken words create your destiny, do not expect to be elevated until you have mastered your mouth.

> *"Let the words of my mouth and the meditation of my heart be acceptable in Your sight,*

oh, Lord, my strength and my Redeemer"
(Psalm 19:14 NKJV).

'Acceptable' words are in alignment with what God says about you and the product of a surrendered heart.

"For out of the abundance of the heart the mouth speaks. A good man out of the good treasure of his heart brings forth good things, and an evil man out of the evil treasure brings forth evil things" (Matthew 12:34b-35 NKJV).

The heart that regularly receives the Word of God cannot help but speak what you have hidden there.

"Your word have I hidden in my heart, that I might not sin against you," (Psalm 119:11 NKJV).

AN ALTERNATE DESTINY

E levation is a lifelong process; but arriving at your Promised Land does not necessarily take that long. Words can be used to determine the length of your journey.

Less than a year after leaving Egypt, the Israelites arrived at the border of the land God had promised to Abraham. In fact, the covenant vow between God and Abraham became the very basis of their religion, history and culture. Yet, as they stood at the precipice of this bountiful land where they would spend the rest of their days, something tragic happened. They doomed themselves to forty years of wandering in one of the most hostile environments on earth—simply because of their negative words.

THINK IT, SAY IT, BE IT

T he land of Canaan was God's *gift* to His people. By just following His directions, they could drink from wells they had not dug, reap a bountiful harvest they had not planted, and live in houses they had not built, on land they had not purchased. What an incredible gift!

Twelve spies went on a forty-day mission to spy out the land. All returned with glowing reports about Canaan, but ten of them added a negative, pessimistic postscript:

> *"The land through which we have gone as spies is a land that devours its inhabitants, and all the people whom we saw in it are men of great stature. There we saw the giants (the descendants of Anak came from the giants); and we were like grasshoppers in our own sight, and so we were in their sight"* (Numbers 13:32b-33 NKJV).

The significance of this verse is most evident in its progression: they **thought** they were weak and insignificant; they **said** they were weak and insignificant; they **became** weak and insignificant.

How strange that the entire adult population chose to believe what ten frightened spies had reported about the 'weak' adults, rather than what Almighty God had promised to give His people!

GO JUMP IN THE OCEAN!

Something is sure to stand between you and your elevation. Promotion can never come as the result of your own efforts. You must trust God to help you complete the journey.

> *"'Have faith in God,' Jesus answered. 'Truly I tell you, if anyone says to this mountain, 'Go, throw yourself into the sea,' and does not doubt in their heart but believes that what they say will happen, it will be done for them'"* (Mark 11:22-23 NIV).

Mountains have many shapes and forms: marital strife, health problems, financial woes, addictions, etc. If you do not know what to speak to your mountain, it will continue to stand squarely in your path.

Every syllable that you speak to your mountain must come from God's Word. So, fill your mind and heart with His words and then tell your mountain to go jump in the ocean!

THE LAST WORD

When you pray, God hears and responds by sending His Word. So, what kind of changes should you expect? How about . . . seasons, circumstances, healing, restoration, alignment, and salvation!

> *"Then they cried to the Lord in their trouble, and he saved them from their distress. He sent out His word and healed them; He rescued them from the grave"* (Psalm 107:19-20 NIV).

The most powerful Word you can ever speak is the name of Jesus. God's Word was the first word and will be the last (John 1:1-2). At the proclamation of His Word, every knee will bow and every tongue acknowledge the sovereignty of God (Romans 14:11). His exalted Name will scatter your enemies, heal your body, calm your heart, secure your future, and save your soul.

Just believing in Jesus' death and resurrection alone will not save you. Another step is necessary:

> *"'The word is near you; it is in your mouth and in your heart,' that is, the message concerning faith that we proclaim: If you declare with your mouth, 'Jesus is Lord,' and believe in your heart that God raised him from the dead, you will be saved. For it is with your heart that you believe and are justified, and it is with your mouth that you profess your faith and are saved"* (Romans 10:8b-10 NIV).

Salvation demands that you open your mouth and send a soul-saving, elevating word into your world!

ON THE MOUNTAINTOP!

Words spoken from a human mouth submitted to God's authority are more powerful than the

> ### Salvation demands that you open your mouth and send a soul-saving, elevating word into your world!

'Big Bang' theory.[19] Words can create, sustain, and transform. Like a nuclear warhead, sending words of praise from submitted lips have an impact upon spiritual dimensions. This is your quintessential element of spiritual authority!

With His human voice, Jesus spoke into the cosmos and declared that His restorative work was completed: *"It is finished"* (John 19:30 NIV). Like the voice of Christ, you possess the power, authority, and responsibility to speak His Kingdom into existence today. Not just for yourself, but for a world in dire need of salvation.

All creation is waiting for the church to open her mouth and send forth words of restoration to establish Christ's completed work . . . "on earth as it is in heaven" (Matthew 6:10). Your ultimate elevation is to stand on the mountaintop, glorify and praise the name of the One who brought you there, and call all creation out of darkness to His eternal light!

---

[19] The Big Bang is the most widely accepted scientific theory of the creation of the universe. http://en.wikipedia.org/wiki/Big_Bang